TABLE OF CONTENTS

I0025589

MEDIA REVIEW

First published by Lawrence Erlbaum Associates, Inc., Publishers
10 Industrial Avenue
Mahwah, New Jersey 07430

Transferred to digital printing 2010 by Routledge

Routledge

270 Madison Avenue
New York, NY 10016

2 Park Square, Milton Park
Abingdon, Oxon OX14 4RN, UK

EDITOR'S CORNER

Greetings all! It is with great pleasure and gratitude that I open these pages of Educational Studies, Volume 37, No. 1. This issue commemorates the 50th anniversary of *Brown v. Board of Education of Topeka, Kansas.* I am grateful on many different levels: first, to the children, families, civil rights activists, and lawyers who made that decision possible; second, to the members of the Supreme Court who had the courage to stand up and make the decision; and last, to all the school personnel and community members who supported the students who first ventured out to take those often-treacherous steps into formerly all-White schools. What an incredible, albeit contradictory and difficult, accomplishment.

I am also very grateful to the guest editors of this issue who worked to bring this issue into being. Sandra Winn Tutwiler and Dianne Smith first approached me a few years back with the idea to put a special issue on *Brown* together. What a great idea! I was happy to help them do so, and they went off to work on it. As is usually the case with these special issues, it wasn't until just this week that I got a chance to really see what they had put together, and wow! What a superb job they have done. This issue is filled with insight, passion, clear and critical analyses, and really moving descriptions of the events surrounding this landmark decision that changed the educational and social landscape of this country—for better and for worse. There are articles, book reviews, an interview, photographs, and a media review in this issue—all coming together to chronicle this 50th anniversary and telling a complicated and contradictory tale. I am certain that many of you will want to use this issue in your classes; I surely will.

There is of course much that could be said about the Brown decision, but rather than take up your time with my thoughts, I will let you dive into the pieces collected here. I feel privileged to have been a part of collecting them here. Thanks so much, again, Sandy and Dianne and all the contributors. I know you worked hard (especially in the end!) to get this issue together, and I appreciate the care and time you put into selecting just the right combination of pieces.

And now, I get to go on vacation! I am off to Cape Breton for a bit of R and R. When you get this issue, we will be buttoning up our overcoats! But not today. Today, it's 91 degrees in the shade here in the Midwest. Time for some sweet Atlantic breezes and a cheap novel. My best to you all!

Rebecca Martusewicz
Editor

INTRODUCTION

The Contradictions of the Legacy of Brown v. Board of Education

DIANNE SMITH
University of Missouri-Kansas City

SANDRA WINN TUTWILER
Washburn University

On May 17, 1954, the Supreme Court ruled that separate school facilities were inherently unequal and thus unconstitutional and illegal. Today, 50 years after this landmark decision, much debate surrounds the efficacy of the ruling, particularly for its impact on the education of children of color in U.S. schools. In reality, *Brown v. Board of Education of Topeka, Kansas*, was never solely about education; neither did the case include only plaintiffs from Topeka. Both points are important to note as we reflect on the legacy of *Brown* a half century after the ruling.

Although legal challenges to segregation in schools took place as early as 1849, political and legal activity to ensure educational equity took on increased fervor following the 1896 *Plessy v. Ferguson* decision, which legalized racial segregation in all sectors of public life. The *Brown* case was preceded by more than 70 years of legal challenges to racial segregation in schooling. The legal success of *Brown* has been heralded as a milestone in the educational history of African Americans, given the promise that school desegregation would improve educational possibilities for African American children and youth. Even so, on-going debates on the nature of educational experiences, achievement, and attainment of African American children and youth have called into question the true cost and benefits of school desegregation.

Brown included 200 plaintiffs, from Delaware; Kansas; South Carolina; Virginia; and Washington, DC. In each case, with the exception of Kansas, plaintiffs sought remedies from grossly inadequate facilities, and in some cases, the training and salaries of teachers were at issue. Separate facilities were far from equal in schools located in these southern states. In contrast, segregated schools in Topeka were well constructed, and African American teachers were well educated. That *Brown* was the lead case accentuated the point that even where facilities and

Headlines (*Source*: Kansas State Historical Society)

Ross Elementary School Staff, Topeka, 1949 (*Source*: Kansas Collection, University of Kansas Libraries)

Monroe Elementary School, Topeka, Kansas (*Source:* Kansas State Historical Society)

First Grade, Washington Elementary School, Topeka, Kansas (*Source*: Kansas Collection, University of Kansas Libraries)

teacher training were ostensibly similar, separate schooling could never be equal. If separate could never be equal for public schools, then separate could never be equal for any public facility. As a result, a ruling in favor of the plaintiffs would lead to the dismantling of the legal basis for "separate but equal" for all sectors of public life.

It is fitting that the articles and book and video reviews included in this special edition of *Educational Studies* focus on personal, social, political, and educational issues prior to and following the ruling in *Brown*. In so doing, we face the fact that the impetus for *Brown* extended well beyond the perceived negative impact of African American children learning in classrooms with children—and, in many cases, teachers—who looked just like them. The legacy of *Brown* implores us to reflect on failures and successes following this historic decision, not only within the context of the education of African American and other children of color but also for other aspects of public and private life this ruling promised to impact.

Correspondence should be addressed to Dianne Smith, University of Missouri–Kansas City, School of Education, 5100 Rockhill Road, Kansas City, Missouri 64110. E-mail: smithdia@umkc.edu

ARTICLES

Forces for Failure and Genocide: The Plantation Model of Urban Educational Policy Making in St. Louis

BRUCE ANTHONY JONES
University of Missouri–Kansas City

This article is about policy decision making and racial politics in the St. Louis, Missouri, school district. From a research standpoint, traditional policy-making models are inadequate for explaining the evolution of school reform events in St. Louis over the past year. Teachers, principals, school staff, and parents perceive themselves to be under siege by an external corporate entity. Within a 4-week period, this corporate entity shut down 16 schools (14 were in the predominantly northside African American neighborhoods); laid off teachers and principals, terminated maintenance, security, and food service staff; and outsourced whole service divisions. One high-performing African American school was shut down and sold to St. Louis University so that the university could bulldoze the school to build a basketball stadium. According to one parent interviewee, "We did not know what hit us."

Table top theory and the plantation model of policy design, development, and implementation are used as conceptual and practical guides to detail the corporate takeover reform experiment in the St. Louis school district. This study demonstrates that policy practices that are detrimental to the well-being of African American children continue to plague African American communities. New methods for understanding why these policy practices continue require extensive discussion and a critical need for changing the way the powers that be interface with African American interests.

> In my many years as a school administrator no one has ever asked me my opinion about how to improve the schools.
>
> —St. Louis African American school principal (2003)

In the 50-year aftermath of the U.S. Supreme Court's decision in the *Brown v. Board of Education of Topeka, Kansas*, case, the United States is in many ways is more segregated racially, ideologically, and geographically than ever (Kozol 1991;

Willis 1994; Jones 1997; Weiler 1998). As recently as 1999, research by Saprotio and Laureau clearly documented how European American families avoid schools that house populations that are more than 20 percent African American, despite the fact that these schools may be high performing, with excellent reputations and facilities. This research also revealed that European American parents prefer poor-performing White schools even if these schools have poorer children with lower test scores than African American schools.

Since the *Brown* decision, wholesale sections of the African American community have moved from poverty status to *structural* poverty status,[1] while as a collective, urban school systems have suffered from high teacher and administrator turnover; high student mobility; dilapidated building infrastructures; and woefully inadequate human, fiscal, and material resources to meet all of the needs of the diverse student populations. Additionally, urban school districts and children in these districts are common targets of curriculum and governance experimentation. Edison Schools, Education Alternatives, charter school proponents, and voucher school proponents, to name a few, constantly vie to secure lucrative contracts to operate individual urban schools or urban school districts. At the expense of children and their families, urban school systems are faced with an unending and vicious cycle of inadequate resources, misappropriation of resources, and experimentation.

The St. Louis, Missouri, school district is no exception, particularly with regard to these last problems. From the perception of many teachers and administrators, the district is under siege. In April 2003, the newly elected St. Louis school board conferred a $5 million contract to the New York-based turnaround corporation Alvarez and Marshall[2] to take over the curriculum, governance, and finances of the school district. The corporation immediately named a former Brooks Brothers executive as interim superintendent. Within a four-week period, the interim superintendent shut down sixteen schools and laid off more than 2,000 school personnel, including teachers, maintenance, security, and food service staff. He also outsourced whole service delivery departments. For example, in November 2003, with the sanction of the school board, the interim superintendent awarded a five-year, $55 million contract to Sodexho, Inc., to take over the district's custodial and facilities division and awarded a four-month (March–June 2004), $7.2 million contract to Aramark Corporation to take over the district's food operations. The latter contract was conferred despite knowledge that Aramark had been linked to food poisoning incidents at other educational facilities and correctional institutions across the country. In the first month of Aramark's operation, cafeteria food service was suspended in thirteen schools in the St. Louis school district because of reported incidents of students becoming ill. Despite this, the school board has held on to the option of renewing the Aramark contract for the 2004–2005 school year at a disclosed amount of $16.3 million.

Racial tensions in the city have been severely heightened by the actions of the school board in contracting with Alvarez and Marshall, because the lay community was not involved in the decision to hire the turnaround firm, and the firm, as well as the interim superintendent, has ignored pleas from the lay community for more community deliberation in its policy decisions. Furthermore, fourteen of the sixteen schools that were shut down were located in the predominately African American north side of St. Louis. One high-performing, predominantly African American school (Waring Elementary) was shut down and sold to St. Louis University so that the university could bulldoze the school to build a basketball stadium. According to one interview account, the interim superintendent, with the backing of near-unlimited resources from Alvarez and Marshall, operated so quickly and swiftly that school teachers, administrators, and local parents did not know what hit them.

This article is about power, politics, and control in the St. Louis educational policy arena: who has it and who does not. How did the St. Louis school district become the first school district in the United States to experience governance by a corporate-turnaround firm? What political conditions precipitated the takeover? What can we learn about politics and educational policy from this kind of urban school reform strategy, and what are the implications of these lessons for future studies on school desegregation and urban school systems in America? With these key questions, in this article I explore how racism, class disparity, conflicting educational policy cultures, and financial self-interests intersect to provide the basis for what I refer to as a *siege and conflict* political and policy study. The *plantation model* of policy design, development, and implementation is used as the primary conceptual guide for this study (Jones 2003).

Researchers for the study conducted 14 one- to three-day site visits to St. Louis between June 2003 and February 2004 to engage in data collection for the siege and conflict study. One-on-one interviews (averaging one hour) were conducted with a purposeful sample[3] of sixteen St. Louis school district teachers and school administrators.[4] In addition, a survey was administered to twelve of the sixteen teacher and administrators who were interviewed. Observational and archival data were collected as researchers attended and documented two school board meetings; three central office meetings; and three community gatherings of parents, politicians, representatives of community-based organizations, religious institutions, the media, and political activists. Researchers also collected local newspaper and electronic mail accounts of the activities of the school board, corporate-takeover firm, and community activists. Pertinent internal central office memos, which were circulated within and outside the school district, were also collected from interview participants. Prior to the site visitations, the researchers developed interview, survey, and observation protocols to ensure that data were collected in a systematic and consistent fashion. Both interview and survey administrations occurred during the regular school day. Generally, survey instruments were left with the sample of teachers and administrators and retrieved on subsequent site visits.

Research Conceptual Guides and Results

Three conceptual guides were used in this study. As Dye (2002, 12) pointed out, political phenomena in the policy arena more often than not are explainable through the overlay of multiple theories, as opposed to a single theory. The first concept, *siege and conflict,* provides the reader with a descriptive understanding of the emotive context of the St. Louis educational policy arena with particular regard to the perceptions of the Alvarez and Marshall firm by school teachers and administrators in the study. The second concept, *table top theory,* serves as a guide for mapping policy structures (or institutions), multiple constituencies (or key players), and the sociopolitical context (i.e., race, class, gender, culture, finance) of the corporate-turnaround school reform strategy. With this conceptual guide, a heavy emphasis is placed on understanding the impact of both *formal* forces—that is, what is readily visible and on top of the policy table—as well as *informal* or covert forces from underneath the policy table that may help explain policy development in complex organizations such as the St. Louis school system. Once data from participants in the study were applied in accordance to table top theory, patterns emerged that seemed to show what I refers to as a *plantation* style of decision making in the St. Louis school community, which is the third concept for this study. Unlike most policy models, the *plantation model* of policy design, development, and implementation places high significance on understanding how history and issues of race affect the policy process. As Cooper, Fusarelli, and Randall (2004) reported:

> The failure to consider adequately the *(forces* of) history and context leads to a poor conceptualization of the policy process …. (for example) How could one even consider school reform for inner-city African American students without knowing the history of slavery, Jim Crow, Reconstruction, civil rights and the culture of the black family? Yet repeatedly, policy "solutions" are offered that ignore the history and context of education problems, presenting them as if new and discovered. (6)

Siege and Conflict

Bal-Tal (2000) discussed something known as the *Masada complex* with regard to societies and institutions that perceive themselves to be under hegemonic attack. From ancient Jewish history, the word *masada* refers to the defense of the Masada from Roman attack and invasion. The Jewish defenders of Masada collectively decided to commit suicide rather than allow themselves to fall into the hands of the Roman enemy. Over time, this episode in history has come to symbolize Jewish heroism and unity in the face of the outside enemy. Today, the *Masada complex* is used more broadly to apply to a collective of individuals and institutions that per-

ceives or actually is under siege by some outside force. Three elements are characteristic of groups or individuals with a Masada complex: (a) a *perception element*,
the tendency to view the outside world as hostile or threatening to the institution;
(b) an *action element*, occurs when the external entity engages in some form of real
action that is viewed as threatening; and (c) a *historical element*, which centers on
the tendency of the institution under siege to cite longstanding historical "proof"
that the external or threatening entity cannot be trusted.

In St. Louis, all three elements of the Masada complex are evident. The interim
superintendent, Alvarez and Marshall, and the mayoral-driven school board are
viewed by school personnel as threatening; this is the perception element. The interim superintendent and school board have adopted policies (i.e., shutdowns of
schools, terminations, layoffs, and outsourcing) that are viewed as threatening; this
is the action element. Last, African American school personnel have provided example after example whereby African Americans have been unjustly treated in St.
Louis, and the actions of the interim superintendent, Alvarez and Marshall, and
school board are viewed as a part of a long chain of negative events that have had a
devastating impact on the community; this is the historical element. The revela-
tions by interviewees that there is a tradition of assault on the African American
community is well supported throughout the literature on the history of St. Louis
(Lipsitz 1991; Stuart-Wells and Crain, 1997; Early 1998; Clamorgan 1999; Kimbrough and Dagen 2000).

Although St. Louis has a remarkable history of education innovation, African
Americans, as a collective, have not been beneficiaries of this remarkable history.
For example, St. Louis was the first locality in the United States to design, develop,
and implement kindergarten. During the mid-1800s, the city was the first to systematically develop alternative educational programs for German immigrants as a
method to assimilate the immigrants successfully into the St. Louis political econ-
omy. In contrast, the St. Louis school board (as with most school boards and state
legislatures across the country) made it illegal to educate African American children. According to Lipsitz (1991), "No person shall keep or teach any school for
the instruction of Negroes or mulattoes." (103)

A more recent and contentious policy action felt by African Americans occurred approximately 20 years ago. The action concerned a current school board
member who is a former St. Louis mayor. During his mayoral campaign he promised that he would reopen a medical hospital (Homer G. Phillips Hospital) that had
a long-standing and significant history of serving the African American community.[5] Once in office, he betrayed the African American community by refusing to
reopen the hospital, which had been unjustly shut down by his predecessor.[6]

A most recent school example of siege and betrayal that is consistent with the
Homer G. Phillips history is the closure of Waring Elementary School during fall
2003. According to an interviewee, "[Waring] was a high-performing school that

served a predominantly African American student population and it was shut down and demolished to build a basketball arena for a predominantly white university (St. Louis University)." Interestingly enough, the former mayor and current school board member who reneged on his promise to reopen the Homer G. Phillips Hospital was reportedly deeply involved in the perceived unjust closing of Waring Elementary School.

Given the policy history just described, many teachers and administrators view the interim superintendent, Alvarez and Marshall, and the school board as comprising the outside force or hostile enemy. Consistent with the Masada complex, one interviewee reported that "We must do what we can to surround our children and protect them from the destructive nonsense of the board and central office."

Table Top Theory

According to Dye (2002), there exists a common thinking that "policy does not become public policy until it is adopted, implemented and enforced by some (public) government entity" (12). This is exactly why traditional theories and models that are used to explain political and policy phenomena are inadequate for this study of the St. Louis school district. This study revealed, from the perspectives of the participants, that policy making can be highly private and exclusive and may unfold in exact contrast to the common thinking described by Dye. In the St. Louis case, policy design often had its roots in private self-interests as opposed to public interests. Furthermore, government entities were used simply to carry out these private interests.

This study used what is referred to as *table top theory* to map key policy structures, multiple constituencies, and the sociopolitical context of activities within and outside the school district. I define *table top theory* as understanding policy as largely a privately driven activity (particularly as this relates to the intersection of private interests and large-scale community control) that uses public or governmental entities as symbols and pawns to carry out said private interests.

In the context of the United States, race, ethnicity, gender, class, culture, and finance are key influential variables in understanding the power and influence of private interests in the educational policy arena. These variables have varying levels of significance depending on the policy issue. Figure 1 illustrates a requirement to examine not just formal public sector forces (i.e., central office, school board, city hall, and public-acting nonprofits) but also informal and less obvious private sector forces (i.e., corporate, business, philanthropic, and some private-acting nonprofits) on urban school reform in the St. Louis district. In the interviews, informal influences on the policy process in the district, the business, and media sectors emerged repeatedly in significance.

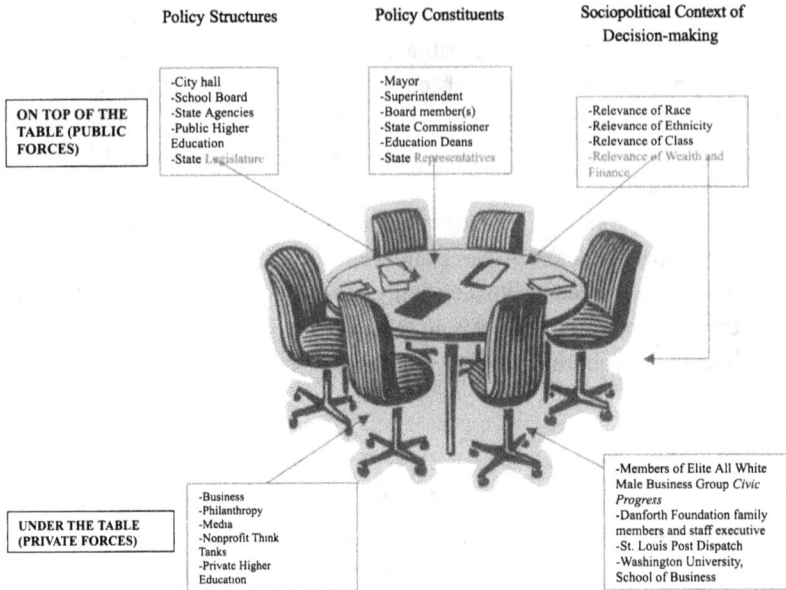

| Policy Structures | Policy Constituents | Sociopolitical Context of Decision-making |

| ON TOP OF THE TABLE (PUBLIC FORCES) | -City hall
-School Board
-State Agencies
-Public Higher Education
-State Legislature | -Mayor
-Superintendent
-Board member(s)
-State Commissioner
-Education Deans
-State Representatives | -Relevance of Race
-Relevance of Ethnicity
-Relevance of Class
-Relevance of Wealth and Finance |

| UNDER THE TABLE (PRIVATE FORCES) | -Business
-Philanthropy
-Media
-Nonprofit Think Tanks
-Private Higher Education | -Members of Elite All White Male Business Group *Civic Progress*
-Danforth Foundation family members and staff executive
-St. Louis Post Dispatch
-Washington University, School of Business |

FIGURE 1   Table top theory schematic: Urban school policy structures, multiple constituencies and sociopolitical context.

Informal Impact of Business

There is no question in the minds of the interviewees that it was informal or private-sector forces that spearheaded the move toward the adoption of turn-around strategies within the district. One interviewee made it clear that "nothing (large-scale) happens in St. Louis without the sanction of the business community." In St. Louis, elite business community interests are represented by Civic Progress, Inc. (Hardy, Dohm, and Leuthold 1995).[7] The business community's informal decision to wrestle control of the St. Louis school district from the African American community was decided several years ago, according to this interviewee: "It is no coincidence that in 1997, the Missouri State Legislature approved the reduction of the school board from 12 to seven members. This reduction paved the way for Civic Progress to easily install its four puppets (using the Mayor[8] to do so) as the majority on the school board." Indeed, school board campaign finance data revealed that the chief companies that comprise Civic Progress contributed significantly (more than $200,000[9]) to the four candidates who won the school board seats in April 2003. The mayor contributed an additional $50,000 to the four candidates from his mayoral campaign fund.

Informal Influences of the Media

The key St. Louis newspaper (*St. Louis Post-Dispatch*) in the city has "never been supportive of the black community," according to one interviewee. Other interviewees expressed their dismay at the lack of balance in the coverage of the events surrounding the actions of the interim superintendent, Alvarez and Marshall, and the school board. "Clearly," another interviewee reported, "the *Dispatch* is on the side of the takeover company—we are being victimized by a reign of terror and the paper is in on it."

The sentiment regarding the relationship between the *Post-Dispatch* and the African American community has historical merit. Newspapers with wide distribution, such as the *Post-Dispatch*, often serve as the major source of information about the business of what is going on in a given community. For many, reading is believing. Newspapers are powerful venues for the distribution of knowledge to the lay public. They are powerful in what they print, how they choose to print information, and what they choose not to print.

A historical example of the power of print centers on the African American struggle for civil rights in St. Louis. Most Americans and historians are unaware of the fact that the first civil rights lunch counter sit-ins in the United States occurred in St. Louis in 1947, 13 years before the Greensboro, North Carolina, sit-ins, yet the history books credit Greensboro as the origin of sit-ins in the United States. According to Kimbrough and Dagen (2000, 7), the decision by the editors of the *St. Louis Post-Dispatch* to not cover the sit-ins in 1947 led to the omission of this civil rights history from U.S. historical memory. A retired *Post-Dispatch* reporter revealed in 1990 that as a young reporter in 1947 he was eager to report on the lunch counter sit-ins but was told by his editor, "The newspaper knows all about it and there's no need for a story."

More than 50 years later, from the perspective of the interviewees, the *St. Louis Post-Dispatch* has not changed. According to a school principal, "Grassroots community, teacher and administrator perspectives about this management company [Alvarez and Marshall] simply are not covered in the *Post-Dispatch*—the coverage has been woefully inadequate and unbalanced."

Philanthropy

Interviews and archival data (newspaper and electronic mail reports) make it clear that representatives of the Danforth Foundation[10] held, and continue to hold, enormous influence over the development of urban education reform in St. Louis. As with Civic Progress, one survey respondent revealed that "the Danforth Foundation is viewed as the big gorilla in town—they've got the money and power to get what they want when they want it despite what local parents think." One individual with enormous behind the scenes informal influence is a former Danforth Foundation executive. This executive is cited as the one individual who is responsible for the creation of the four-person (mayoral-backed) school board slate that won the school board election in 2003. As previously pointed out, collectively these four individuals constitute the school board majority and are responsible for hiring the firm Alvarez and Marshall and approving all actions of the firm.

This former Danforth Foundation executive is credited with investing in the design and development of what is known as the *Vashon Compact*. The Vashon Compact is touted as a neighborhood-improvement initiative involving six elementary schools, three middle schools, a newly constructed high school, and an entire newly constructed housing/apartment complex.

Interviewees held mixed views about the Vashon Compact. For some, the compact represented the ideal kind of partnership among education, business, and philanthropy. For others, the compact represents a noose around the neck of the school district because it exists at the expense of other schools in the district that are not receiving the same level of attention or investment. Moreover, critics contend that the compact is more hype than substance because the compact schools are not performing any better than other schools in the district.

Plantation Model of Policy Design, Development, and Implementation

After mapping the key policy structures, multiple constituencies, and policy context through the use of table top theory, I developed a policy model that appears to explain what is going on in the St. Louis school district with respect to the relationship between the multiple constituencies and the urban school reform initiative. This explanation is grounded in what I refers to as the *plantation model* of policy design, development, and implementation. There are seven characteristics of the plantation model of policy design, development and implementation:

1. Although the policy issue centrally concerns a *historically disenfranchised group* (e.g., African Americans, Native Americans, women, etc.) the process is *European American* and *male* driven.

In St. Louis, the school district is predominantly African American (82 percent), but decisions are being driven by European American men. The publicly stated policy issues focus on the academic achievement of African American children. In particular, there is concern with whether the school district can close the achievement gap between African American and European American children.

2. In contrast to collaboration and distributive leadership, the policy process is *hierarchal* and top-down.

More than one half of the interviewees expressed disgust over losing the focus on site-based management when Alvarez and Marshall and its representative interim superintendent began running the district. According to an interviewee, "The previous administration had a staff person who was devoted to assisting the schools to implement site-based management. One of the early personnel actions of the interim superintendent was to eliminate this person and his job along with the site-based management philosophy." Another interviewee reported, "[Alvarez and Marshall] came down on us with a heavy foot." A third interviewee reported that the Alvarez and Marshall team from New York adopted a "micromanagement approach to school restructuring—we were told what to do, when to do it, but often not how to do it." This same interviewee complained that "staff members were moved and principals had no say in who they got [as replacements]." One principal reported that the prior administration allocated budgets to the schools (basically at the beginning of the school year) and left it up to the schools to decide how to allocate the budget. In contrast, the turnaround firm allocated budgeted amounts to the schools monthly in order to sustain tight control over the resources. The principal at one school reported on the devastating impact on the school left by the elimination of the site-based management philosophy: The schools had to give up decision making that was contextual in nature and abide by generic policy actions and decisions that were not necessarily appropriate for all schools; enrichment programs for kids were slashed or eliminated because the turnaround firm had no understanding of the significance of these programs; and (c) resources to pay teachers for extra service activities afterschool were eliminated. As a result, some teachers agreed to participate in after-school activities without compensation. Also, resources for professional development were virtually eliminated. Professional development is not a priority under the current management company. Moreover, "It appears the current company does not know how to serve our professional development needs."

3. In contrast to respect for a diversity of viewpoints, the policy process in the plantation model is characterized by extreme *arrogance, indifference,* and *paternalism.* Consistent with paternalism, there is this tendency in some policy circles to "go up to the plantation attic" to retrieve what is usually a White male retiree to serve as a consultant or advisor to the policy initiative. Being old, White, male, retired, and connected ("the old boy network") are often the only collective credentials these individuals need to have to serve in these roles.

Several interviewees felt that the actions of the interim superintendent, Alvarez and Marshall, and the school were arrogant and paternalistic. One interviewee complained that "Principals are not respected as human beings or as professionals. The district is driving away urban teachers." A teacher complained that "[Alvarez

and Marshall] don't seem to care that our best and brightest are leaving the city."
The departures, according to this interviewee, are occurring because there is uncer-
tainty about job stability within the district, those leaving are young and don't
know how deep the budget cuts will be, and the morale in the schools is low—this
(the St. Louis school district) is not a good place to work. Ultimately, according to
the teacher, "This will have a negative impact on student academic performance
and overall teacher efficacy."

Two of the interviewees reported that the height of arrogance and paternalism
occurred when the interim superintendent and his staff offered two free school outfits to parents who ensured that their children came to the opening school day in
September 2003. According to the interviewee, parents were informed that after
they dropped their children off at school they could proceed to the local Goodwill
thrift store to retrieve the two free (and previously owned) outfits for their children.
This interviewee reported, "It's a bit presumptuous on the part of the interim superintendent, who is from Brooks Brothers clothing, to assume that we [largely African American parents] shop at Goodwill."

4. The policy process and its impact on the historically disenfranchised group
    is *unpredictable*. There is no rhyme or reason or logical way to figure out
    how policy decisions are made.

This factor appeared repeatedly as the most major concern among the school
administrators and teachers who were interviewed and surveyed. Several interviewees reported that the failure of the interim superintendent and the school board
to plan long-term program strategies for the district fueled an environment of un-
predictability. One interviewee complained that he was sick and tired of being told
by central office that "something is due on Thursday on Wednesday." He reported,
"They need to sit down and engage in the simple task of planning." Another interviewee stated, "There is an uneasy climate in our building due to so many issues
the district is facing—we don't know what is going to happen." A teacher reported
that "there is massive confusion surrounding procedures and routines in the district. Under previous administrations, this was so clear."

5. The policy process is *punitive* in nature. From day to day, the reality faced
    by victims of the plantation model is wrought with anxiety and fear. For ex-
    ample, individuals may be suddenly terminated from their jobs without
    reason or due process.

There is no question in anyone's mind that the turnaround firm will not hesitate
to use punitive measures for school staff who do not go along with the firm's policy
actions. Two individuals refused to participate in this study: One was afraid that

she might lose her job, and the other individual was afraid that he might be over-looked for a job promotion. One interviewee confirmed that "This governing body [Alvarez and Marshall] has everyone afraid of losing their livelihood. Working in fear is definitely not good." A teacher reported that she believed her principal has been cut out of the central office loop because the principal dared to question the actions of the superintendent.

6. The policy process is highly *inconsistent.* The employment of *C.A.R.* (Concepts, Actions, Reality) in policy analysis is a useful tool for understanding what is meant by policy inconsistency. *C.A.R.* is concerned with what "drives" a policy initiative with regard to: the underlying *concepts* that are publicly expressed as a means to explain the policy initiative, *actions* that are used to implement the policy initiative, and the *reality* of experiences faced by individuals who are the beneficiaries or victims of the policy initiative. Figure 2 provides a basic illustration of how a policy can be inconsistent. In the United States, the Bill of Rights broke down between the underlying concepts of the document and the actions by policymakers with the reality of life faced by African Americans. This inconsistency had, and continues to have, brutal consequences for African Americans in the United States.

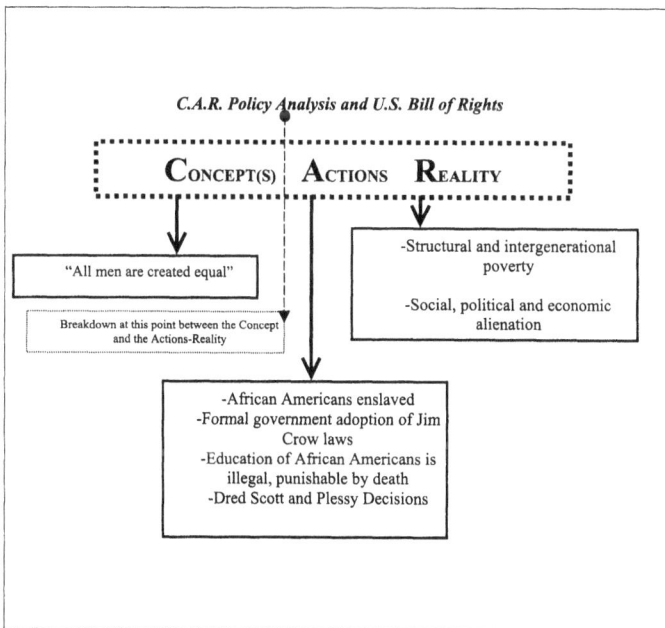

FIGURE 2   C.A.R. policy analysis and the U.S. Bill of Rights

Several justifications for the policy actions of the school board and the superintendent have been expressed to the public. Initially, the policy actions were taken under the guise of a reported $99 million deficit faced by the St. Louis school district. However, a state audit revealed that the district did not have a $99 million deficit and that the school board violated state law by passing an unbalanced budget in 2003. Low student achievement has been cited as another reason for the actions of the school board and turnaround firm. However, the data over a three-year period showed that student drop-out rates, graduation rates, and achievement rates (at the elementary and middle school levels) were trending in the right direction. On the basis of the achievement data, the district needed not a hostile takeover but rather assurance that policy actions by the school board would remain consistent with the trend data. As one principal pointed out, "All of our work has been completely knocked off track."

7. Levels of decision-making authority within the plantation model are driven by racial considerations. There are three levels of individual decision-making authority that are possible with the plantation model of policy design, development, and implementation: individuals who possess *mandate* authority, individuals who possess *advisory* authority, and individuals who possess *symbolic* authority. Individuals in the policy arena who hold mandate authority hold absolute authority; in other words, what they say goes. Individuals who function at an advisory level hold minimal decision-making authority, and individuals who operate at a symbolic level hold little, if any, decision-making authority in the policy process. In addition, the data in Table 1 contend that there is an inverse relation between levels of racial diversity in the policy arena and levels of authority. In other words, as authority increases toward the "absolute" category, racial diversity decreases.

It is clear, from the perspectives of all of the interviewees, that principals and teachers have had zero authority over decisions that have emanated from central office and have had a direct impact on the schools. In fact, according to one interviewee, "We don't even play in token roles downtown."

Table 1 outlines the levels of authority that key constituents have in the St. Louis corporate-turnaround strategy for urban school reform. According to the table, the

TABLE 1
The Plantation Model and Decision-Making Manifestations

Multiple Constituencies (Individuals)	Levels of Racial Diversity	Levels of Decision-making Authority
Individuals with *mandate* authority	Zero (or near)	Absolute
Individuals with *advisory* authority	Moderate (racial tokenism)	Minimal
Individuals with *symbolic* authority	High (racial tokenism)	Zero

mandate level of authority is dominated by representatives of both the private and public sectors. Although levels of authority vary within this level, all of the political actors are White men. This means the worldview through which policy manifests for the largely African American children and their families in the St. Louis community is a White male worldview.

Business and Philanthropy

It was very clear to over one half of the interviewees that the business and philanthropic communities hold mandate authority over decision making within the St. Louis educational policy arena and other policy arenas in the city. As has already been pointed out, "No decisions are made without the sanction of the elite business membership organization, Civic Progress, Inc."

The work of Civic Progress and the Danforth family influence in St. Louis go hand in hand. Over the years, Danforth family members have served as the leading

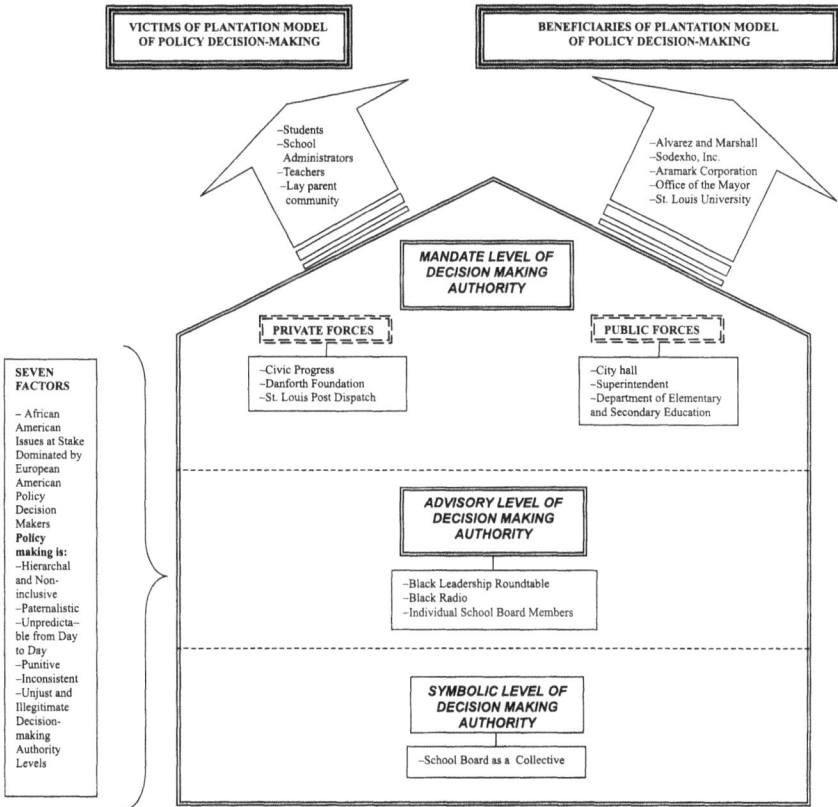

St. Louis Black Leadership Roundtable Decision-Making Authority

FIGURE 3   The plantation model schematic: Victims and beneficiaries.

roles in Civic Progress, Inc. The Danforth Foundation leads one of the most heavily private supported education initiatives in the city (the Vashon Compact). Moreover, has been reported, a former Danforth Foundation executive led the movement to put the current school board majority in place with the support of the St. Louis corporate community and the mayor's office. The Danforth influence, although not known by everyone, is clearly at a mandate level of decision-making authority.

Consistent with the plantation model template, African Americans begin to hold some level of decision-making authority in the St. Louis educational policy arena only at an advisory level. Individuals who hold a mandate authority of decision making may or may not abide by the advice of African Americans who operate in the educational arena at this advisory level. For example, the St. Louis Black Leadership Roundtable (BLR) is a powerful force in regard to sociopolitical and economic issues that affect the African American community in St. Louis. However, despite this power, this group does not hold mandate authority. In fact, throughout the tenure of the corporate-turnaround actions of the interim superintendent, school board, and Alvarez and Marshall, and the subsequent community turmoil, the BLR remained strangely silent. This silence was eventually broken when a local African American popular radio talk show host began reading the names of the BLR members on her radio show. She also, in essence, began exposing and labeling the BLR members as traitors to the Black community for not standing up to what was perceived as an assault on the education of African American children in the St. Louis community. In some quarters, members of the BLR were being referred to as "handkerchief heads" and "Uncle Tom"s.[11]

The advisory (as opposed to mandate) level of decision-making authority of the BLR was evident when on July 21, 2003, the group issued a press release demanding that the corporate and mayoral-backed school board and interim superintendent rescind the decision to close the sixteen schools in St. Louis. The press release read, in part: "There are several unanswered questions as it relates to the process in which 16 schools have been selected and determined to close. The process leading to the decision is fatally flawed." The BLR advice was completely ignored, and the sixteen schools were immediately shut down.

School Board Decision-Making Authority

In a textbook sense, the school board as a collective is supposed to hold a mandate level of decision-making authority. However, on the basis of observational and archival data, no school board member held a mandate level of decision-making authority, and certain school board members appeared to serve at an advisory level of decision-making authority while others were simply at a symbolic level of authority. It appeared very clear from the beginning of the school board term, in June 2003, that the interim superintendent, who reported to Alvarez and Marshall, had near-complete autonomy to run the district. It appeared that he directed the school board, as opposed to the other way around. Therefore, contract outsourcing, school personnel layoffs, and school closures appeared to occur with minimal input from the school board. At one point, relations between the interim superintendent and a member of the school board (who was not a part of the four-person mayoral slate) deteriorated into a shouting match. The latter had to remind the interim superintendent that he works for the school board and that the school board does not work for the interim superintendent.

The ongoing influence of the office of the mayor and the business community appeared to diminish the decision-making authority of the school board. As previously indicated, the four-person majority of the school board was put in place with the vital financial support of Civic Progress and the mayor. Finally, at least two interviewees expressed concern that no member of the school board had children who attended the St. Louis public schools. In addition, no member of the school board came from the public education sector. In this regard, some interviewees believed that the school board authority was diminished because the members lacked knowledge about the legal authority they had to run the district.

Conclusion

This study clearly demonstrates how structural barriers that are driven by economic self-interests, arrogance, and paternalism can cause massive failure in an urban education system. These self-interests view urban schools systems as consulting cash cows and venues for consulting firms to engage in unending cycles of educational experimentation at the expense of African American children and their families. Given this, the St. Louis School District was ripe for the picking. Several interviewees for this study revealed that the corporate takeover of the school district appeared to have been in the making for a number of years. Although the school district is predominantly African American, the plantation model of policy design, development, and implementation provides a primary conceptual framework for demonstrating how predominantly European American power structures dominate and control the education of African Americans, who have little power and authority over decision making in the school district. Private-sector corporate and philanthropic interests set the stage for the corporate takeover, which became the first of its kind in U.S. history.

This study confirmed that no discussion of urban education politics and policy should occur without recognition of the salient role of racism. The plantation model of policy design, development, and implementation sheds light on how forces for failure and genocide can thrive in urban education systems that are hierarchal, arrogant, paternalistic, unpredictable, punitive, inconsistent, and racist in their decision-making attributes. Children cannot learn, and adults cannot thrive, in school systems that are run like plantations. The biggest challenge for the

St. Louis school district will be to break out of the shackles that are characteristic of a plantation policy model and into a governing and educationally sound system that is viewed by the indigenous African American community as politically credible, inclusive, and participatory.

Unfortunately, on the occasion of the 50th anniversary of the *Brown vs. Board of Education of Topeka, Kansas*, decision, many organizational and policy decision-making elements of the St. Louis school district are in deep disrepair. Teacher and administrative morale is at an all-time low, and many are questioning whether they have a future in the district. The school climate is all the more worse with the recent and untimely death of St. Louis civil rights activist Minnie Liddell. Liddell is the individual who filed the landmark 1972 lawsuit, on behalf of her son, Craton Liddell, that challenged the school district's desegregation strategy. Her legal challenge led to the nation's most expensive school desegregation settlement.

The 1954 *Brown* decision and the work of civil rights pioneers such as Liddell left an enduring positive legacy. However, much more work needs to be done to eliminate the plantation model of governance in urban education systems. From the perspectives of the teachers and administrators, this study revealed that the corporate takeover of the St. Louis school district was a dismal failure. This sentiment is consistent with a recent newspaper account (Simon, 2004): "The consultants will return to New York in June 2004, their $4.7 million contract up. They will leave behind a school district in chaos—and a city enraged."

Notes

1. Individuals who are in a state of *structural* poverty have lost faith in the major institutions of society. These institutions—for example, schools, universities, city hall, police and justice departments, and so on—do not work for them and have no legitimacy. This sentiment, over time, leads to *system disengagement* and is perpetuated from generation to generation. According to Jones (1994), *system disengagement* (to be distinguished from *apathy*) is a legitimate self-protection measure internalized and acted on by individuals who perceive that they are under siege by the political system. The political system is hostile toward said individuals and simply does not work for them. See also Triandis's (1988) concept of *ecosystemic distrust syndrome,* whereby extreme poverty, discrimination, and social rejection undermine the credibility of any social or political system. In contrast, individuals who are in a state of poverty (as opposed to structural poverty) have not yet lost faith in the system and still believe, for example, that education is the way out of economic poverty.
2. Alvarez and Marshall is a New York-based turnaround firm that secures contracts with struggling companies attempting to avoid or come out of bankruptcy. The St. Louis school district is the company's first foray into the education arena.
3. *Purposeful sampling* is the identification of sites or individuals for a particular study that will best help the researcher understand the problem or research question (Creswell 2003, 185).
4. The sample included teachers and administrators who were transferred from schools that were suddenly shut down by decree of the takeover firm (Alvarez and Marshall); in highly effective schools that were characterized by high student academic performance, as measured by the Missouri Assessment Program; and in low-performing schools that were char-

acterized by low student academic performance as measured by the Missouri Assessment Program examination.

5. Homer G. Phillips Hospital was the first comprehensive-service hospital in St. Louis to serve the African American community. In addition, the hospital served as a training ground for many St. Louis practicing doctors, nurses, and medical personnel. The hospital was also a chief employer within the African American community.

6. After the shutdown, the hospital stood abandoned for several years. In 2002 the building was converted into a senior citizens' facility.

7. Civic Progress, Inc., founded in 1953, consists of (European American) businessmen who lead the largest corporations in the St. Louis region. It has been referred to as the "shadow government" of St. Louis as it is used as a venue to craft policy for government and serve private economic interests.

8. In June 2003, following the April school board elections and the hiring of the turnaround firm (Alvarez and Marshall), newspaper accounts referred to the newly elected four-member majority on the school board as "Slay's raiders," named after the mayor, Francis Slay.

9. According to newspaper accounts, these companies included Anheuser-Busch, Ameren, Emerson Electric, and Energizer Eveready Battery.

10. The Danforth Foundation was established in 1927. Investments by the foundation have historically focused on what the foundation believes to serve the best economic, scientific, and educational interests of the St. Louis region. The assets of the foundation are reportedly in excess of $355 million.

11. These names are directed toward African Americans who are viewed as doing some level of harm to the African American community. *Uncle Tom*, for example, means "Black on the outside but White on the inside." In the plantation model, these African Americans would be referred to as *house Negroes*, who spy on the activities of Blacks enslaved in the field and report these activities back to the White master. Throughout U.S. history, African American insurrection and protest have been thwarted by individuals acting as "house Negroes."

References

Bar-Tal, Daniel. 2000. *Shared Beliefs in a Society: Social and Psychological Analysis.* London: Sage Publishers, Inc.

Clamorgan, Cyperian. 1999. *The Colored Aristocracy of St. Louis.* Columbia: University of Missouri Press.

Cooper, Bruce S., Lance D. Fusarelli, and E. Vance Randall. 2004. *Better Policies, Better Schools: Theories and Applications.* Boston: Pearson Education.

Creswell, John W. 2003. *Research Design: Qualitative, Quantitative and Mixed Methods Approaches.* Thousand Oaks, Calif.: Sage Publications.

Dye, Thomas R. 2002. *Understanding Public Policy.* Englewood Cliffs, N.J.: Prentice Hall.

Early, Gerald. 1998. *Ain't But a Place: An Anthology of African American Writings About St. Louis.* St. Louis: Missouri Historical Society Press.

Hardy, Richard J., Richard R. Dohm, and David A. Leuthold. 1995. *Missouri Government and Politics.* Columbia: University of Missouri Press.

Jones, Bruce A. 2003. School leadership in siege and conflict. Paper presented at the annual meeting of the American Educational Research Association, Chicago.

Jones, Bruce A. 1994. "Schools in the Community and Urban Context: Incorporating Collaboration and Empowerment." In *Investing in U.S. Schools: Directions for Educational Policy,* edited by Bruce A. Jones and Kathryn M. Borman, 5–18. Norwood, N.J.: ABLEX.

Jones, Bruce A. 1997. "Desegregation: Education, Politics and Policy Legacies." *Negro Education Review* XLVIII: 109–119.

Kimbrough, Mary, and Margaret W. Dagen. 2000. *Victory Without Violence: The First Ten Years of the St. Louis Committee of Racial Equality (CORE), 1947–1957.* Columbia: University of Missouri Press.

Kozol, Jonathon. 1991. *Savage Inequalities.* New York: McGraw-Hill.

Lipsitz, George. 1991. *The Sidewalks of St. Louis: Places, People, and Politics in an American City.* Columbia: University of Missouri Press.

Saportio, Salvatore and Annette Lareau. 1999. "School Selection as a Process: the Multiple Dimensions of Race in Framing Educational Choice." *Social Problems* 46:418–438.

Simon, Stephanie. "St. Louis Roiled by School Turnaround Gambit." *LA Times,* March 14, 2004.

Stuart-Wells, Amy, and Robert L. Crain. 1997. *Stepping Over the Color Line: African American Students in White Suburban Schools.* New Haven, Conn.: Yale University Press.

Triandis, Harry C. 1988. "The Future of Pluralism Revisited." In *Eliminating Racism: Profiles in Controversy,* edited by Phyllis A. Katz and Dalmas A. Taylor, 31–50. New York: Plenum Press.

Weiler, Jeanne. (1998). *Recent Changes in School Desegregation.* New York: ERIC Clearinghouse on Urban Education.

Willis, H. D. (1994). The shifting focus in school desegregation. Paper presented to the Southwest Regional Laboratory (SWRL) Board of Directors and at the 1995 Equity Conference.

Correspondence should be addressed to Bruce Anthony Jones, University of Missouri–Kansas City, School of Education, 5100 Rockhill Road, Kansas City, Missouri 64110. E-mail: Jonesba@umkc.edu

The Unfinished Agenda of School Desegregation: Using Storytelling to Deconstruct the Dangerous Memories of the American Mind

LOYCE CARUTHERS
University of Missouri-Kansas City

This article describes school desegregation as a 3-generational, intricately linked process. The 1st generation included efforts toward physical desegregation for African American students; the 2nd generation emphasized equal access to classrooms, teaching bias, and ability groups; and the challenges of the 3rd generation include barriers to equal education outcomes. Dangerous memories of school desegregation are interwoven with historical and sociocultural precepts that have helped to shape schooling in America, including ideas about individualism, merit, cultural superiority, equality, and abundance of economic opportunity. Thus far, school desegregation has failed because many educators have not examined beliefs and assumptions about cultural differences. The unfinished agenda of the 3rd generation persists amidst the complexities of the first 2 generations. The dangerous memories of school desegregation that permeate our minds may be transformed through storytelling. I demonstrate the strategy using the story of an urban school educator, almost 5 decades after *Brown v. Board of Education of Topeka, Kansas* (1954), and offer suggestions to help educators implement storytelling in their schools.

Dangerous memories run deep and wide, decentering our very being and, like stories, memories are the core of culture. Quinn (1992) noted that culture includes everything that makes us who we are—beliefs, assumptions, theories, and stories; it comprises people enacting a story and living in ways that make the story a reality. Memories, as a process of "cultural production" (Giroux 1994, 31) and often removed from historical, social, and political context, can provide opportunities for us to open up rather than close history. In this article I evoke the dangerous memories of school desegregation that involve complex constructs of race/ethnicity, class, and gender. I examine the unfinished agenda of the third generation of school desegregation and introduce storytelling as a staff development tool for reflecting and acting on the conditions of schooling in America. Race and ethnicity are included because each has its own distinct history in America. Also, there is ample evidence that school policies toward second-language learners are related to complex issues of power and control in U.S. society.

The evolving quest for equal educational opportunities has been depicted as a three-generational process (Network of Regional Desegregation Assistance Centers 1989). Efforts toward physical desegregation for African American students are viewed as first-generation problems; second-generation problems are characterized as equal access to classrooms, teaching bias, and ability grouping. The persistent barriers to equal education outcomes are challenges of the third generation. Some educators and researchers have labeled the current barriers to equal education outcomes as an *achievement gap* that exists between disenfranchised students, such as African Americans and Latinos, and their more advantaged peers (Williams 1996). Today, the problems of three generations, intricately linked, continue in a society where there is silence about race/ethnicity, class, and gender; people act as if there are no differences (Hernandez 1997). We fail to collectively name and claim differences in achievement as "things that we, together, have both produced and allowed" (Pollock 2001, 10).

Current educational reform movements, especially in urban districts, espouse democratic ideas and reordered relations among teachers and administrators under the guise of improved teaching and learning. Unfortunately, these efforts often fail to address enduring historical and philosophical ideologies about race/ethnicity, class, and gender that are entangled in memories and guide the behaviors and actions of many educators. The "culture of whiteness" (McLaren 1995, 50) is used in the story of American education to frame our meanings and perceptions of cultural difference. The culture of Whiteness emerged from the bedrock of American cultural outlook termed the *Protestant–Republican ideology* (Adams 1995, 13–14) and included:

The sacredness and fragility of the republican polity (including ideas about individualism, liberty, and virtue); the importance of individual character in fos-
tering social mobility; the central role of personal industry in defining recti-
tude and merit; the delineation of highly respected but limited domestic roles
for women; the importance for character building of familial and social environment (within certain racial and ethnic limitations); the sanctity and social
virtues of property; the equality and abundance of economic opportunity in
the United States; the superiority of American Protestant culture; the grandeur
of America's destiny; and the necessity of a determined public effort to unify
America's polyglot population, chiefly through education.

I offer storytelling as a way to talk about the "undiscussables" related to
race/ethnicity, class, and gender. These dangerous memories are those subjects
that people choose not to talk about because they have often been taboo in educational settings. By using stories to begin a dialogue about one's beliefs, attitudes,
and assumptions that affect pedagogy and behavior, schools may begin the long
process of desegregating the minds of educators. *Desegregation* is defined in *Webster's Ninth New Collegiate Dictionary* as "to free of any law, provision, or practice
requiring isolation of the members of a particular race in separate units" (343). To
desegregate the minds of educators and others requires examining dangerous
memories that involve what Anderson (1992) noted as "grand," "master," and
"meta" narratives consisting of assimilation ideologies and monocultural perspectives of Anglo conformity, varying forms of social and economic middle classism,
and the perennialism of the melting pot philosophy. These dangerous memories
through stories often influence the structure and organization of schooling and cast
poor and culturally diverse children as "other." To be cast as "other" means "to experience how the dominant meanings of a society render the particular perspective
of one's own group invisible at the same time as they stereotype one's group and
mark it out as the other" (Young 1990, 59).

I acknowledge that breaking the silence around the undiscussables will not fix
the three generations of complex desegregation issues U.S. society faces. Yet our
voices must be used to resist narratives that control our lives in schools. We also
must work with others to interrupt social practices and structures, linked to larger
societal meanings that appear to be beyond our control. To illuminate for the reader
the intertwining of memories and stories in the shaping of culture, I deconstruct
my own dangerous memory of school desegregation. Alcoff (cited in Collins 1990,
4) defined the process of deconstruction as "exposing a concept as ideological or
culturally constructed rather as a natural or a simple reflection of reality." I follow
this story with a description of the unfinished agenda of the third generation of
school desegregation. The use of storytelling as a staff development tool is discussed and the process demonstrated with a story of a high school administrator of
an urban school, almost five decades after *Brown v. Board of Education of Topeka,*

Kansas (1954). Storytelling, if used critically and framed within historical, social, and political context, can help educators become more aware of beliefs and assumptions about differences and work collectively to promote actions that challenge the problems of the third generation. Fifty years after *Brown*, I turn to a deconstruction of my dangerous memory of school desegregation.

The Aftermath of *Brown*

I was raised in Kansas City, Missouri, sixty miles from the Topeka, Kansas, courthouse. I began kindergarten in 1952, when segregated schools were a way of life. All my classmates and teachers looked like me. Back then we did not call ourselves *African Americans*; to many of us, "Africa" was Tarzan and Jane avoiding the "wild savages," the Africans. We knew very little about our African heritage and our contributions to the world. I left the safety of a segregated community in 1961 when my mother moved to the south part of town and, for the first time, I attended a majority White school. I quickly learned that avoiding the wild savages— the "Black kids" was also another rendition of Tarzan and Jane but this time played by White teachers and students who fought physical desegregation. The Black students had their own special entrance, the back door of the school, which represented the segregated Black community. The letter grade C became a special signet for "colored people," and we did not expect a grade above a C. These are just a few of the countless dangerous memories of behaviors and practices of school desegregation that influenced my life. I came to understand that memories shape our thinking and thus our behavior. When you treat people as inferior, they begin to act inferior. Some are able to rise above these perceptions and manipulate the system rather than succumb to rumors of inferiority.

For a short time during my teenage years, I found ways to numb my pain of being the other through the use of self-destructive behaviors and acts of resistance. Eventually, I was able to forge an identity and a comfortable space for living out a different reality with the help of a few teachers who believed that I was worthy of teaching. Becoming somebody meant submerging my culture and hiding from the "face of difference," trying to fit into a world that viewed cultural differences as deficits and valued Eurocentric ways of thinking and behaving. The words of bell hooks (1992) express the pain of my collective dangerous memories:

> Without a way to name our pain, we are also without the words to articulate our pleasure. Indeed, a fundamental task of black critical thinkers has been the struggle to break with the hegemonic modes of seeing, thinking, and being that block our capacity to see ourselves oppositionally, to imagine, describe, and invent ourselves in ways that are liberatory. Without this, how can we challenge and invite non-black allies and friends to dare to look at us differently, to dare to break their colonizing gaze? (2)

My memories of school desegregation are continuously interpreted and reinterpreted as I interact with the memories and pain of other people with similar experiences. Fifty years after *Brown*, these memories have been recast in the same geographical location where any gains in desegregation have been rapidly lost. Kansas City's schools, like those in other cities, are becoming increasingly segregated. In Kansas City, Missouri, African American students continue to attend largely segregated schools; 2003 state data report that 70.66 percent of the 33,855 students in the Kansas City, Missouri, school district are African American (Missouri Department of Elementary and Secondary Education 2003). These figures are typical of other school districts with enrollments greater than twenty-five thousand (Frankenberg and Lee 2002) where African American and Latino students attend largely segregated schools. "The literature suggests that minority schools are also associated with low parental involvement, lack of resources, less experienced and credentialed teachers, and higher teacher turnover—all of which combine to exacerbate educational inequality for minority students" (Frankenberg and Lee 2002, 5).

Orfield, Eaton, and the Harvard Project on School Desegregation (1996) concluded that the Supreme Court decisions of the 1990s were not about how to further desegregation but how to dismantle it. They further contended that "by allowing for the dismantling of special programming for segregated schools, the 1995 Supreme Court Decision, *Missouri v. Jenkins*, suggests that the Supreme Court will not even support enforcement of the 'separate but equal' doctrine that *Brown* overturned" (xv). The intent here is not to debate the status of school desegregation or its trends; the evidence is contrary to the often-dismal conclusions surrounding school desegregation and the myth of its failure.

> In spite of a very brief period of serious enforcement of the law, segregation persisted and increased for decades. The desegregation era was a period in which minority high school graduates increased sharply and the racial test score gaps narrowed substantially until they began to widen again in the 1990s. Most Americans believe that desegregation has substantial benefits and say that more, not less, should be done to increase integrated education (Frankenberg, Lee and Orfield 2003, 67).

The Unfinished Agenda of the Third Generation of Desegregation

The *Brown* decision led the way for dismantling the dual systems of Black and White schools, described as the first generation of desegregation. The limitations of physical integration were apparent some ten years after *Brown* in the attitudes, policies, practices, and programs of desegregated schools. "The second generation came about because schools—sometimes unintentionally—were segregating children by race and by sex within classrooms" (Network of Regional Desegregation

Assistance Centers (1989, 1). Title VI of the 1964 Civil Rights Act was an attempt to deal with second-generation problems related to unequal access to classrooms, teaching bias, and ability grouping. Also realized during this period was the denial of equal access and equitable treatment for language minority students and limited or non-English speakers. Desegregation plans included ways to reduce the physical isolation of students and to address class and program placement issues. Attention was given to gender roles for females and to increase their enrollment in nontraditional courses, such as math and science. Title IX of the 1972 Education Amendments, the Supreme Court Decision of *Lau v. Nichols*, 1974, and the subsequent development of the Lau Guidelines increased the need for expanding the scope of desegregation assistance services (Network of Regional Desegregation Assistance Centers 1989).

As desegregation tasks evolved, it became apparent that physical desegregation and ensuring access through the courts were not adequate. The focus of the third generation of desegregation is on learning and student outcomes. These third-generation problems might be described as the persistent barriers to integration or equity or the attainment of equal education outcomes for all groups of students. Even when physical integration and a reasonable level of equal access is achieved, there exists a differential achievement of students and subtle attitudinal and structural elements that limit equal opportunity (Network of Regional Desegregation Assistance Centers 1989, 10).

Today, fifty years after *Brown,* public schools face problems linked with each of the three generations. The dangerous memories of school desegregation continue to pervade our minds and shape the culture of our schools. The unfinished agenda of the third generation looms largely in the midst of "considerable confusion about the status of desegregation law [that] exists but clearly the basic trend is toward the dissolution of desegregation orders and return to patterns of more intense segregation" (Frankenberg, Lee and Orfield 2003, 20). The problems of the third generation of desegregation, a creation of dangerous memories, can be seen in tracking and ability grouping (Oakes 1992; Wells and Serna 1996); low expectations for student behavior and academic achievement based on race/ethnicity, class, and gender (Paine 1989; Sadker, Sadker, and Steindam 1989; Scott-Jones and Clark 1986; Winfield 1986); and watered down and fragmented curricula for poor students (Moll 1988; Nieto 1992). Poor students and non-Asian minorities are disproportionately enrolled in low-track academic classes, and advantaged students and White students are more often enrolled in high-track classes. Wells and Serna (1996) described tracking and detracking reforms as a struggle over whose culture and lifestyle are valued and whose ways of knowing are equated with intelligence. They further noted that "to the extent that elite parents have internalized dominant, but often unspoken beliefs about race and intelligence, they may resist 'desegregating' within racially mixed schools ... because they do not want their children in classes with Black and Latino students" (96).

The challenges of the third generation require opportunities for educators to deconstruct dangerous memories and make visible beliefs and assumptions about cultural differences. These differences are well hidden within the cultural ways of schools and are often portrayed through teaching methodologies, codes of disciplines, administrative practices, and policymaking. The voice of a White male high school student depicts the hidden transcript of race and his attempt to make meaning of cultural differences:

> I think that differences do matter. If they didn't then everybody would be friends. Everybody would hang out with everybody. People wearing different clothes and hairstyles, it does matter. Everybody sort of naturally have the belief that what they do is the best. People that aren't like you, they don't accept. They will say they accept but when you look at who they hang with, it is people who are like them. I always heard that this was a school of unity, and everyone is accepted; but when you get here, and you are here for a while and interact with different people, you realize that there is a place you are suppose to be. I was expected to hang out with whites because I am white. (Caruthers 1996, 10)

The young man in this story attended a magnet school program designed to attract majority White students. He was starkly aware of how the silence about cultural differences affected the culture of the school. As a benefactor of the first generation, I connected to the experience of a young White male of the third generation because we both experienced the dangerous memory of isolation. Even today, I wonder if this young man had the opportunity to deconstruct his experience with school desegregation. What story will he tell?

Stories Are the Way We Live

"Stories are the way we make sense of our lives: by telling them, we tell ourselves who we are, why we're here, how we come to be what we are, what we value most, and how we see the world" (Colombo, Lisle and Mano 1997, 5). Desegregating our minds involves different ways of seeing and knowing and valuing the experiences of all students. The suppression of personal experiences within schools and teacher education often contributes to the absence of reflective practices, relationships, and overall caring, which tends to reproduce technocratic and corporate ideologies that promote change without difference (Gay 1993; Irvine and York 1995; Wexler 1992). Storytelling, in the context of my work with urban educators, makes use of a deconstruction process that exposes a concept as ideological or culturally constructed rather than a natural or a simple reflection of reality. The power of the strategy is magnified when it is combined with inquiry and dialogue with others around the often-hidden transcripts of race/ethnicity, class, and gender. Participants identify other related topics that emerge from the desire to increase knowledge and skills for during culture work. Storytelling has been used to help teachers think more deeply about the meaning of teaching, learn about teacher socialization, transform teacher–educators' research and practice, and promote school reform (Clandinin 1993; Hollingsworth 1994; Jalongo and Isenberg 1995; McWilliam 1994; Wallace 1996). A critical approach challenges the ways knowledge is constructed; illuminates the relationship between knowledge and power; and redefines the personal and political so that we learn to rewrite the dialectical connection between what we learn and how we come to define our history, experience, and language (Giroux 1992). Concepts that are key to the use of stories are voice, inquiry, and personal knowledge. *Voice* enables us to use our constructed meanings for active engagement in community. Britzman (1990) pointed out that voice implies "the individual's relationship to the meaning of her/his experience and hence, to language, and the individual's relationship to the other (14). *Inquiry* results from questioning and challenging the status quo. "Inquiry is necessary at the outset for forming personal purpose. While the latter comes from within, it must be fueled by information, ideas, dilemmas and other contentions in our environment" (Fullan 1993, 15).

The failures of many educational reform initiatives have come about because "they didn't get at fundamental underlying, systemic features of school life: they didn't change the behaviors, norms, and beliefs of practitioners" (Evans 1996, 5). Most efforts at reform school do not include opportunities for educators to deconstruct dangerous memories that decenter our very being. A White male-dominated majority and middle-class norms and expectations, rather than multicultural perspectives, often shape the schools' curricula and what people value as official knowledge and truth (Belenky et al. 1986; Collins 1990; McLaren 1995). Acquiring *personal knowledge* about race/ethnicity, class, and gender allows us to both affirm and question students' experiences and keep alive the possibilities of desegregating our minds and social transformation. Although I advocate the use of storytelling as a staff development tool for desegregating the American mind, I realize that this strategy alone is not sufficient unless stories also engage broader efforts within the community so that making a difference, according to Fullan (1993), is "explicitly recast in broader social and moral terms ... broader social public purpose (11). I illustrate the approach (Caruthers 2000) through the story of an urban high school administrator's struggle to help a White male teacher deal with many of the problems of the unfinished agenda of the third generation of school desegregation. I demonstrate the use of voice, inquiry, and personal knowledge to deconstruct the story of Karen Jackson and an interview about her story a year later. The deconstruction strategy consists of the following questions: (a) what did I see relative to race/ethnicity, class, and gender? (b) what did I not see about race/ethnicity, class, and gender? (c) why is there silence about race/ethnicity, class, and gender? and (d) why did I see race/ethnicity, class, and gender? In the deconstruction of Karen Jackson's story, I use the descriptors of gender bias and race bias to describe rigid or negative attitudes toward a group or groups that are formed in disregard of facts. Bias is related to discrimination but is different. *Discrimination* entails behaviors that violate federal, state, or local nondiscriminatory human rights or civil rights laws.

Karen Jackson, Vice Principal of an Urban High School

I sat in on an interview for a high school drama/forensics teacher. The candidates who applied for the positions all had impressive credentials. There was one candidate who had very impressive credentials, but all of his work had been done in a small, somewhat rural community in _____. The candidate had a small stature and looked somewhat timid. Why on earth, I remembered thinking, would he want to work in this school? The students would take one look at him and have him for lunch. This particular candidate had numerous reasons why he wanted the position, but the number one reason was he felt he could build an exciting program at our school in the drama and forensics areas.

The principal and I were the interviewing team. Although we both were very impressed with his interview, his physical stature, the lightness in his voice, and lack of experience in working in an urban setting made us somewhat reluctant to offer him the position. Nevertheless, his passion for wanting the teaching position inspired us to give him a try. The first day of class, he was overwhelmed with the language of the students. During the first few weeks at the school, he had to endure quite a bit of name-calling from the students. His classes weren't going very well, and he would visit with me about the culture of the school. He also asked many questions about urban students and how to relate to them. He was very passionate about his subject matter, but he didn't quite know how to relate to his new population of students. We visited for hours on end after school about relating to his new students. I had only one piece of advice for him: "Never let them see you sweat."

In addition to the problems he was having in the classroom were the problems the school was having in general. With a number of personnel changes in the administration and teaching staff of the building there was, to put it bluntly, almost anarchy each day in this school. The drama teacher had never worked in so much chaos and was trying to make sense of it. His first year in our building was truly difficult. He often talked about quitting during the first semester, but something happened. In the second semester, even though he was only five feet and five inches tall, he began to tower over the students. He became more in tune to what was really going on. He began to understand the language of the students, and they began to understand that when you came to his class you were expected to work and learn. He held auditions for his plays. The students were reluctant at first, but the ones who auditioned and were cast in the performances became overnight success stories among the other students. The next time auditions were held, the number of students who where interested in auditions overwhelmed him. A similar thing happened with his forensics class. He chose material to which the students could relate. They began to win a few rounds at the tournaments, then more and more, until they were neck and neck with the suburban schools. The teacher was inspired and decided to come back another year. In his second year, we continued our talks. I think that I became his biggest supporter on the staff, because I really saw that he cared about the students and that he could teach. His classes were in demand the second year he was in our building, and the students continued to blossom onstage. He sought out scholarships in drama for his seniors. He began taking his students out into the community to give them more exposure and to let the community know that there were some good things going on in our school. The students also began to take first place in the forensic tournaments. The newspaper picked up on the great job the kids were doing. This also was a plus and inspiration to the kids. Students kept their grades up so they could participate in tournaments, and they took much pride in being onstage in front of their peers. There was no more name-calling, only respect and love for this teacher. The kids would work exceptionally hard for him because they knew the end product was for them.

Talk about a transformational learner—he was one of the best I have ever seen and with whom I have had the opportunity to work. He did wonders for the self-esteem of the students. Also, the principal supported him in most of his endeavors and this helped his program tremendously. The drama teacher from _____ became an urban teacher to the fullest extent. I wish this story could have had a happy ending, because it was a great success story for the students. The third year for this teacher became a nightmare. A new principal was assigned to the school. The drama teacher and the principal did not see eye to eye. The new principal got rid of the drama teacher by the end of the year. The students were saddened beyond belief. How could the new principal treat this teacher so miserably? What could have been so bad about his teaching?

At the end of the school year, the teacher left, the principal received a promotion, and the drama/forensics department is now back to square one. I can't make any meaning out of this story other than teachers who don't teach and fail large percentages of students appear to be safer than teachers who do teach. Either way, the students in this particular school are losing. They sometimes lose the teachers who teach and lose an education from the ones who don't or can't teach. How sad!

Interview With Karen Jackson

Interviewer (I): When you look at this story today, is there a different interpretation or view about what happened based on the experiences you have had?

Respondent (R): The thing I would add is that this principal was on the fast track. He used his biracial wife for universal appeal. If he sees something Black becoming too strong, he crushes it. He is a user. This teacher was one of the two best teachers in the school. He was a small man and would come and ask for help. He wanted to make the kids the best they could be. The new principal saw what a good job he was doing to promote Black kids. Whenever he saw a teacher interested in Black kids and trying to make them great, the person would be shut down. This teacher used the strength of the kids. You can come into urban schools, but you have to watch who is watching you and whether or not you will be able to make a difference.

I: What do you believe is needed to transform the instructional climate in urban schools?

R: Teachers need a voice that will be heard. They have ideas and want to work. Teachers need more information on how schools have improved. Need to keep abreast of the literature, know what is going on. Parent involvement is key. Schools will not get parents until teachers make a personal commitment. They have to hear something nice about their children. Make parents feel their kids are special. Schools need to become more of a community center. Incorporate more community activities that involve less formality than learning.

Deconstruction of Karen Jackson's Story and Interview

What Did I See Related to Race/Ethnicity, Class, and Gender?

The inexperienced teacher described by Karen perceived that the culture with which he was confronted in his new assignment is strange and different. The students also sensed his fear of the strangeness. The perspective he brought to this strange and different context is a candid view of his shortcomings and a yearning to understand cultural differences. He seemed not to understand that the students may have been alienated from an official curriculum that did not include their histories, lived experiences, interests, and backgrounds. After years of exposure to the dangerous memories of exclusion, the students learned to anesthetize their fears of inadequacy and alienation through the development of a subculture that included ways to gain acceptance from peers.

Humor, distinct ways of communicating and behaving, and even acts of cruelty promoted a subculture of acceptance and belonging within their own peer group. They had learned how to resist. Karen recognized the veiled challenges to the status quo and cautioned her young protégé to "never let them see you sweat." She also viewed this advice as a strategy for desisting negative behavior. She viewed the students' use of language to demean the teacher as cultural phenomenon rather than a reaction to the culture of schooling. Acting-out behavior is often a reaction to students' alienation from the school. High achievement may be associated with "acting White" and buying in to a culture of exclusion.

Through dialogue and deconstructing his stories with Karen, the teacher gained more confidence in his abilities. Karen helped him to establish relationships with the students through using their backgrounds and interests to engage them in school. Students soon learned that he was offering them opportunities for success and to experience schooling in a different way. Unknowingly, she captured the power of storytelling. The stories of both the teacher and students changed in the second semester. They began to live a different reality, seemingly letting go of their old, dangerous memories.

In the interview, Karen added more description to this teacher's unique ability to engage culturally diverse students and described the danger inherent in being an advocate for them. At the same time, she saw the personal risk teachers take when they attempt to change the status quo. "This teacher used the strength of the kids. You can come into urban schools, but you have to watch who is watching you and whether or not you will be able to make a difference." This risk is also named in her story: "Teachers who don't teach and fail large percentages of students appear to be safer than teachers who do teach."

What Did I Not See Related to Race/Ethnicity, Class, and Gender?

In both the story and interview, Karen seemed not to understand the assumptions she made about the teacher's inability to teach Black students because of his size and voice tone. Her reluctance to hire this teacher because of physical characteristics appeared to indicate gender and race bias. She had formulated some expectations about maleness and assumed that a large man with a deeper voice was needed to control and manage African-American students. Karen's dangerous memories influenced her beliefs and assumptions.

The principal and I were the interviewing team. Although we both were very impressed with his interview, his physical stature, the lightness in his voice, and lack of experience in working in an urban setting made us somewhat reluctant to offer him the position. She had difficulty naming the cultural understanding that took place between this teacher and his Black students and did not connect his transformation to school reform. Karen understood the importance of teachers using their voices and being heard and valued, but she did not connect teacher voice to challenging issues of social justice within the school. Instead, she used the values of expert and efficiency, the current language of cognitive reform, during the interview to explain what is needed to transform the instructional climate of urban schools.

Teachers need a voice that will be heard. They have ideas and want to work. Teachers need more information on how schools have improved. they need to keep abreast of the literature, to know what is going on. Karen writes about her frustration with the system but cannot name racial bias as a reason for the demise of this teacher's tenure at the school. During the interview, she talked more about the issues of race/ethnicity, class, and gender—breaking the silence surrounding the undiscussables.

> If he sees something black becoming too strong, he crushes it. He is a user. This teacher was one of the two best teachers in the school ... The new principal saw what a good job he was doing to promote Black kids. Whenever he saw a teacher interested in Black kids and trying to make them great, the person would be shut down.

Why Is There Silence About Race/Ethnicity, Class, and Gender?

Karen's silence about the issues of race/ethnicity, class, and gender may be attributed to the topics being taboo in her school. She did not use her voice to construct meaning about why "teachers who don't teach and fail large percentages of students appear to be safer than teachers who do teach." She recognized the importance of valuing the culture and background of students, but it did not occur to her that efforts to understand cultural differences should be included in school reform.

Why Did I See Race/Ethnicity and Gender?

I was able to recognize issues related to race and gender bias because of my personal and professional experiences in these areas. I was reminded of my own dangerous memories. The assumption that being female or African Americans equips you with the ability to recognize and label sexist or racist attitudes and behaviors is often erroneous. The individual must be able to construct meaning from his or her cultural knowledge and experiences in order to name and understand these areas. The deconstructed story of Karen Jackson represented my constructed reality of race/ethnicity, class, and gender (Caruthers, 2000). I now turn to a discussion of what must take place in schools for the approach to be meaningful and transformative for both of us.

Storytelling as a Critical Stance for Staff Development

The stories of educators contain expectations, assumptions, and beliefs that often have the most to do with what is going on in schools. These instances of their captured lives may portray sociocultural and historical ideologies that have guided the development of American education; including ideas about individualism, merit, equality, an abundance of economic opportunity, cultural superiority, and gender expectations. The subtle and overt messages contained in stories such as

Karen's cannot be fully apprehended and understood unless there are opportunities within the school to inquire and to examine the memories and thinking that shape the attitudes and behaviors of all persons. In other words, we must work to desegregate our minds. Storytelling, as a critical stance for staff development, provides opportunities for educators to delve beneath the surfaces of acts, motives, behaviors, and practices. Topics embedded in this story are the history of school desegregation, culture, and language; the official curriculum; culturally relevant curriculum; identity formation; resistance theory; interpersonal skills development; and ways to create community-based schools that are democratic and self-fulfilling.

To initiate storytelling in schools and the broader study of culture, everyone involved in the effort writes a story about life in school. The story might describe a teaching and learning event, interactions with students and other adults, a discipline issue, special celebrations, or other significant and relevant events. Participants are given the options of identifying themselves or remaining anonymous. Next, the group spends time learning inquiry skills or ways of talking together. The goal is to help the group engage in internal listening, accept differences, and build mutual trust. Participants must suspend judgment, listen, and explore other points of view without resorting to debate. Practicing advocacy and inquiry should be done first with less sensitive topics.

Senge (1990) suggested ways of balancing advocacy and inquiry so that all persons involved confront own and others' assumptions, reveal feelings, and build common ground.

1. When advocating your view, make your own reasoning explicit (How did you arrive at your view; on what did you base it?); encourage others to explore your view (Are there gaps in my thinking? Does it make sense?); encourage others to provide different views (Are there different conclusions, different data, different perspectives?); and actively inquire into others' views that differ from yours (What is your view? How did you arrive at your view? What data are you using to support your view?).

2. When inquiring into others' views, state your assumptions clearly and acknowledge that they are assumptions, state the data on which your assumptions are based, and do not ask questions if you are not genuinely interested in the others' responses.

3. When you arrive at an impasse, ask what data or logic might change the other's view or if there is any way you might together design an experiment or engage in future studies that might provide new information.

4. When you or others are hesitant to express personal views or to experiment with alternative ideas, encourage yourself and other people to think aloud what might be making it difficult (e.g., What is it about the situation, about me, or about others, that is making exchange difficult?). If there is a mutual desire to do so, design with others ways of overcoming these barriers.

Following the use of advocacy and inquiry with less sensitive topics, the facilitator selects two or three stories for small groups to deconstruct. The process consists of the following questions: (a) what did I see relative to race/ethnicity, class, and gender; (b) what did I not see about race/ethnicity, class, and gender; (c) why is there silence about race/ethnicity, class, and gender; and (d) why did I see race/ethnicity, class, and gender. Remaining in small groups, participants take turns discussing the stories and their responses. After each person has had a chance to provide input, participants are encouraged to use advocacy and inquiry skills to explore their own and others' ideas. This process is repeated with other stories. As trust develops among the group members, the facilitator encourages them to bring in stories about their current teaching experiences. The goal shifts to helping the group build new shared assumptions and to begin the process of developing a more inclusive culture in which all learners are understood and valued. Stories are changed from deficit-oriented thinking to ways to improve teaching and learning for all.

Current stories in schools can be changed to those that contain conceptual schemes that are essential to desegregating the minds of educators and creating transformative relationships. Achieving such a goal requires examining dangerous memories and putting the experiences of culturally diverse students and poor students at the center of our thinking. This distinction is the major difference between reformed schools and transformed schools. Although I recognize that this strategy cannot significantly change the lives of many students in the world without making broader structural changes in our society, I believe that each of us has the power to make a difference for kids. Stories can change our inner communication and lead to more equitable behaviors and practices. As a key staff development strategy, storytelling has the power to help others resist the sameness and hopelessness that often confront some educators and to embrace a personal mission of possibilities for all learners.

References

Adams, David W. 1995. *Education for Extinction: American Indians and the Boarding School Experience (1875–1928)*. Lawrence: University Press of Kansas.

Anderson, James E. 1992. "Leadership and training programs for educational improvement." In *Students in At Risk Schools: Improving Environments for Learning*, edited by Hersholt C. Waxman, Judith Walker de Felix, James E. Anderson, and H. Prentice Baptiste, Jr., 137–142. Newbury Park, Calif.: Corwin Press.

Belenky, Mary Field, Blythe McVicker Clinchy, Nancy Rule Goldberger, and Jill Mattuck Tarule. 1986. *Women's Ways of Knowing: The Development of Self, Voice, and Mind*. New York: Basic Books.

Britzman, Deborah. 1990. *Practice Makes Practices: A Critical Study of Learning to Teach*. Albany: State University of New York Press.

Brown v. Board of Education of Topeka, 347 U.S. 483 (1954).

Caruthers, Loyce. 1996. *Paseo Academy of the Performing Arts: Student Interview Results; Technical Report*. Aurora, Col.: Mid-Continent Regional Laboratory.

————. 2000. Raising silent voices: Using stories to transform the culture of urban schools. PhD diss., Univ. Missouri—Kansas City.

Clandinin, D. Jean. 1993. "Teacher Education as Narrative Inquiry." In *Learning to Teach, Teaching to Learn: Stories of Collaboration in Teacher Education,* edited by D. Jean. Clandinin, Annie Davies, Pat Hogan, and Barbara Kennard, 1–18. New York: Teachers College Press.

Collins, Patricia Hill. 1990. *Black Feminist Thought: Knowledge Construction and the Politics of Empowerment: Perspective on Gender* (vol. 2). New York: Routledge.

Colombo, Gary, Bonnie Lisle, and Sandra Mano. 1997. *Framework: Culture, Storytelling and College Writing.* Boston, Mass.: Bedford Books.

Evans, Robert. 1996. *The Human Side of School Change.* San Francisco: Jossey-Bass.

Frankenberg, Erica, and Lee Chungmei. 2002. *Race in American Public Schools: Rapidly Resegregating School Districts.* Cambridge, Mass.: Civil Rights Project, Harvard University. Available online at http://www.law.harvard.edu/civilrights

Frankenberg, Erica, Lee Chungmei, and Gary Orfield. 2003. *A Multiracial Society With Segregated Schools: Are We Losing the Dream?* Cambridge, Mass.: Civil Rights Project, Harvard University. Available online at http://www.law.harvard.edu/civilrights

Fullan, Michael. 1993. *Change Forces: Probing the Depth of Educational Reform.* London: Falmer Press.

Gay, Geneva. 1993. "Building Cultural Bridges: A Bold Proposal for Teacher Education." *Education and Urban Society* 25:285–299.

Giroux, Henry A. 1992. *Border Crossings: Cultural Workers and the Politics of Education.* New York: Routledge.

————. (1994). *Disturbing Pleasures: Learning Popular Culture.* New York: Routledge.

Hernandez, Adrian. 1997. *Pedagogy, Democracy, and Feminism: Rethinking the Public Sphere.* Albany: State University of New York Press.

Hollingsworth, Sandra. 1994. *Teacher Research and Urban Literacy Education: Lessons and Conversations in a Feminist Key.* New York: Teachers College, Columbia University.

hooks, bell. 1992. *Black Looks.* Boston: South End Press.

Irvine, Jacqueline, and Darlene E. York. 1995. "Learning Styles and Culturally Diverse Students: A Literature Review." In *Handbook of Research on Multicultural Education,* edited by James A. Banks, and Cherrie A. McGee Banks, 484–497. New York: Simon & Schuster, Macmillan.

Jalongo, Mary R., and Joan P. Isenberg. 1995. *Teachers' Stories: From Professional Narrative to Professional Insight.* San Francisco: Jossey-Bass.

McLaren, Peter, 1989. *Life in Schools: An Introduction to Critical Pedagogy in the Foundations of Education.* White Plains, NY: Longman.

————. 1995. "White Terror and Oppositional Agency: Towards a Critical Multiculturalism." In *Multicultural Education, Critical Pedagogy, and The Politics of Difference,* edited by Christine E. Sleeter and Peter L. McLaren, 33–70. Albany: State University of New York Press.

McWilliam, Erica. 1994. *In Broken Images: Feminist Tales for Different Teacher Education.* New York: Teachers College Press.

Missouri Department of Elementary and Secondary Education. 2003. "Annual Report of School Data." Available online at http://www.dese.state.Mo.us/schooldata/four/048078/demonsone.html

Moll, Luis C. 1988. "Some Key Issues in Teaching Latino Students." *Language Arts* 65:465–472.

Network of Regional Desegregation Assistance Centers. 1989. *Resegregation of Public Schools: The Third Generation.* Washington, DC: U.S. Department of Education.

Nieto, Sonia. 1992. *Affirming Diversity: The Sociopolitical Context of Multiculutural Education.* New York: Longman.

Oakes, Jeanne. 1992. "Can Tracking Research Inform Practice? Technical, Normative, and Political Considerations." *Educational Researcher* 21:12–21.

Orfield, Gary, Susan Eaton, and The Harvard Project on School Desegregation. 1996. *Dismantling Desegregation: The Quiet Reversal of* Brown v. Board of Education. New York: New Press.

Paine, Lynn. 1989. *Orientation Toward Diversity: What Do Prospective Teachers Bring?* (Research Report 89-0). East Lansing: Michigan State University, National Center for Research on Teacher Learning.

Pollock, Mica. 2001. "How the Question We Ask Most About Race in Education Is the Very Question We Most Suppress." *American Educational Research Journal* 30:2–11.

Quinn, Daniel. 1992. *Ishmael.* New York: Bantum/Turner.

Sadker, Myra, David Sadker, and Sharon Steindam. 1989. "Gender Equity and Educational Reform." *Educational Leadership* 46 (6) 44–47.

Scott-Jones, Diane, and Maxine L. Clark. 1986. "The School Experiences of Black Girls: The Interaction of Gender, Race, and Socioeconomic Status." *Phi Delta Kappan* 67:520–526.

Senge, Peter M. 1990. *The Fifth Discipline: The Art and Practice of the Learning Organization.* New York: Doubleday.

Wallace, David K, ed. 1996. *Journey to School Reform: Moving From Reflection to Action Through Storytelling.* Washington, DC: National Education Association.

Webster. 1985. *Webster's Ninth New Collegiate Dictionary.* Springfield, Mass.: Merriam-Webster.

Wells, Amy S., and Irene Serna. 1996. "The Politics of Culture: Understanding Local Political Resistance to Detracking in Racially Mixed Schools." *Harvard Educational Review* 66:93–118.

Wexler, Philip. 1992. *Becoming Somebody: Toward a Social Psychology of School.* Washington, DC: Falmer Press.

Williams, Belinda, ed. 1996. *Closing the Achievement Gap: A Vision to Guide Change in Beliefs and Practices.* Alexandria, Va.: Association for Supervision and Curriculum Development.

Winfield, Linda. 1986. "Teacher Beliefs Toward At-Risk Students in Inner-Urban Schools." *The Urban Review* 18:253–267.

Young, Iris Marion. 1990. *Justice and the Politics of Difference.* Princeton, N.J.: Princeton University Press.

Correspondence should be sent to Dr. Loyce Caruthers, 5100 Rockhill Road, Kansas City, Missouri 64110-2499. E-mail: CaruthersL@umkc.edu

The Impact of Brown on African American Students: A Critical Race Theoretical Perspective

CRAIG A. SADDLER
Miami University of Ohio

There is no doubt that the 1954 *Brown v. Board of Education of Topeka, Kansas*, Supreme Court decision was instrumental in initiating monumental change in the ways public schools have operated. The central question addressed by the Supreme Court in the *Brown* cases (1954, 1955) was whether segregation of children in public schools solely on the basis of race deprives minority children of equal educational opportunities even when all else is equal. The author suggests that the problems faced by African American students are complex and convoluted when contextualized in traditional notions of effective schooling. Such is the case because African American students are filtered into lower educational tracks at such a rapid pace and are often the unfortunate victims of mis-education. The author uses *critical race theory* to deconstruct the historical as well as contemporary resistance offered to the full implementation of the *Brown* decision.

How we have arrived at the present state of affairs can be understood only by studying the forces effective in the development of Negro education since it was systematically undertaken immediately after emancipation. To point out merely the defects as they appear today will be of little benefit to the present and future generations. These things must be viewed in their historical setting. The conditions of today have been determined by what has taken place in the past, and in a careful study of this history we may see more clearly the great theatre of events in which the Negro has played a part. We may understand better what his role has been and how well he has functioned in it. (Woodson 1933, 9)

The problem of educating Black children in America is as old as the presence of Blacks within this country. This complex issue has been the topic of discussion by many notable scholars. Dr. Carter G. Woodson, Dr. W. E. B. Dubois, Marcus Garvey, Dr. Janice Hale, Dr. Martin Luther King, Jr., and a host of others have all asserted that an *effective* education is of fundamental importance in the progress of African Americans. However, the abundance of reports that indicate the systematic and rapid rate at which African Americans are filtered into lower educational tracks suggests that the dominant culture within U.S. society has a different definition of *effective* than these notables. Existing inequities and suggested contemporary solutions (e.g., the current voucher debate and the No Child Left Behind legislation) cause me to wonder about the future of public education.

Woodson's (1933) opening quote affirms that in order to obtain a full understanding of the current state of affairs in education, one must acknowledge the historical events that set the stage so long ago—an essential step in engaging in critical discourse. Although in this article I do not revisit the education of African Americans as far back as emancipation, I do attempt to illuminate the central theme of persistent struggle for liberation in the history of the education of Black Americans. In the first part of this article I provide a brief overview of critical race theory (CRT). I use the theory as my primary lens to deconstruct the aftermath of the landmark case *Brown v. Board of Education of Topeka, Kansas* to critically analyze the degree to which the ideals Thurgood Marshall forwarded during his arguments have been realized.

Theoretical Lens

In my opinion, very few philosophical discourses adequately speak to the impact that the construction of race has on the power relations within U.S. culture as well as the greater geopolitical society.[1] White supremacy has permeated into numerous societal structures, such as law, and is poised to continue the marginalization and subordination of people of color. I believe that this reality in large speaks to the need to emancipate those on the margins and that the following three themes embedded within CRT attempts to provide this liberating effect.

The first theme of CRT states that racism is a normal part of American society. Delgado (1995) asserted that this theme calls attention to the reality that racism is a normal daily fact of life in society and that the dogmatic assumptions of racism are so deeply ingrained in the political and legal structures as to be almost unrecognizable. The strategy of those who fight for social justice is to unveil racism in all of its variations. This task can be somewhat challenging because not all forms of racism are easy to detect and identify. Oftentimes, racism is ingrained into systematic structures (e.g., schooling) and must be unveiled layer by layer. The second theme challenges the experience of White European Americans as the normative standard. CRT grounds its conceptual framework in the distinctive contextual experiences of people of color and racial oppression through the use of literary narratives and storytelling to challenge the existing social construction of race. Tate (1996) argued that the stories of persons of color come from a different frame of reference and therefore give them a voice that is different from the dominant culture and one that deserves to be heard. Critical race theorist Gloria Ladson-Billings (1999) argued that that to appreciate one's perspective, that individual's voice must be understood. The third theme attacks liberalism and the natural belief in the law to create an equitable, just society. CRT advocates have pointed to the frustrating legal pace of meaningful reform that has attempted to eliminate blatant hateful expressions of racism and has gone as far to suggest that liberal legal practices support this lethargic pace (Delgado 1995).

CRT can be a powerful lens through which to investigate the current state of affairs in public education today, fifty years after *Brown,* when schools are more segregated than ever. Before the *Brown* decision, Blacks were knocking on the schoolhouse door demanding entrance into all-White enclaves. In 2004, diversity has a new look both in the inner cities as well as in suburban America. The equal opportunities fought for during the fifty years after *Brown* have given way to what appears to be an inevitable de facto segregation in urban America. This discussion examines the progress (or lack thereof) contemporary public schools have made in an effort to provide equal educational opportunities for African Americans. The phenomenon of resegregation or the entrenchment of original segregation is explored in the sections to follow.

Black Students and School Failure

According to Hale (1986), an important component of education for the disenfranchised should include education for liberation. To this end, Black history in America cannot be separated from the attempt to handle the challenge of Black education in this setting of historical oppression. Too often, Black children suffer in schools because school staff, who have the power to label, classify, and define, do not always have our children's best interest at heart. Lerone Bennett (1972) contended:

> He who controls images controls minds, and he that controls minds has little or nothing to fear from bodies. This is the reason why Black people are not educated or are mis-educated in America ... The system could not exist if it did not multiply discrimination ... An educator in a system of oppression is either a revolutionary or an oppressor ... The question of education for Black people in America is a question of life and death. It is a political question, a question of power ... Struggle is a form of education—perhaps the highest form.

The inescapable reality has been, and continues to be, that the liberation of African Americans is dependent on an effective education. The term *effective* is critical, because so much of our education has been virtually useless in accomplishing the objective of liberation. Over seventy years ago, Woodson (1933) asserted that the process of "mis-education" has impeded the progress of African Americans. He argued that the majority of "educated" Blacks were all but worthless in the liberation of their people in that their education was too basic and technical and had not prepared them to critique their own condition. Unfortunately, his analysis remains an issue of deadly accuracy today—that the issue at hand is how and what African Americans are being taught.

Today, we can argue that African American youth are not only mis-educated but actually "de-educated." The term *de-educated* is used to shed light on the fact that, as a whole, African American youth are being systematically excluded from the education system and/or being systematically destroyed within that system. One needs only to examine the statistical trends of present educational practices to validate this assertion. According to the College Board (1985) and the Carnegie Quarterly (1984/1985), Black students, even if they attend schools with Whites, receive an education that is different and inferior. Their data revealed that Black students, particularly Black male students, are three times more likely to be in a class for the educable mentally retarded than are White students but are only one half as likely to be in a class for the gifted or talented. Also, Black students are more likely than White students to be enrolled in general and vocational tracks and take fewer academically rigorous courses. Only thirty-three percent of Blacks are enrolled in college preparatory classes, compared with fifty-two percent of Asians and forty percent of Whites.

Even more recently, Education Trust, Inc. (2004) reported that in 2003, nationally, fourth-grade African Americans lag behind their White peers in reading. More specifically, 61 percent of fourth-grade African Americans recorded below-basic scores in reading compared to 26 percent of fourth-grade White Americans. Conversely, 12 percent of fourth-grade African Americans recorded proficient to advanced scores compared to 39 percent of fourth-grade White Americans.[2] Similar statistics are reported in eighth-grade mathematics. Education Trust, Inc. also reported that in 2003, 61 percent of all African Americans in eighth grade reported below-basic scores in math. However, only 21 percent of all eighth-grade White Americans reported below-basic scores. On the other hand, only 7 percent of all African American eighth-grade students reported proficient or advanced scores in math, compared with 36 percent for White American eighth-grade math students. These discrepancies also continue into higher education. For example, according to the 2002 NCAA Division I Graduation Rates, 41 percent of African American college freshman graduated within 6 years (NCAA Division 1), compared with 61 percent of White American college freshmen.[3]

These, as well as other glaring statistics illuminating the failure of Black students in public education, cause me to ask "What is the purpose of schooling?" According to Kowalski and Reitzug (1993), the purpose of schooling can be best explained by analyzing the relation between schools and society. This close-knit relationship serves three important roles: (a) to transmit and preserve the existing culture, (b) to respond to changes in society by adjusting curricula and instruction as appropriate, and (c) to serve as an agent of societal growth or improvement. In addition to this definition, when investigating the politics in educating Black children, Atkinson and Hord (1983) stated:

> Every educational system functions to perpetuate the larger society by
> acculturating its young into that order, and the purpose of the American colonial
> education system is to maintain this societal structure. Its claims of individual
> freedom, cultural pluralism and world democratization obscure its ideologies of
> elitism, cultural monism, and world Americanization; and Black children are
> the acculturated victims ... These cultural realities contribute to the academic
> and cultural problems of Black students; mis-educated to believe in individual
> freedom, and that one is thus responsible for one's own success or failure. Black
> students often question their own intelligence when they do not succeed in
> school. (3–4)

When investigating the previously mentioned purpose of schools as presented
by Kowalski and Reitzug (1993), a claim can be made that the first (to transmit and
preserve the existing culture) and third roles (to serve as an agent of societal
growth or improvement) have historically been in conflict. Analyzing the purpose
of schools following the *Brown* decision perhaps provides the best illustration of
this phenomenon.

Through storytelling, I will attempt to illustrate *Brown*'s impact on a fictitious
African American male, Frantz. It is important to note that although the characters
are not real, the events described are real and are all too familiar to many African
American families. From a CRT perspective, epistemology looks at how one
knows reality as well as the method for knowing the nature of reality. For researchers working from within CRT, the way of knowing reality is to ask about it (i.e., via
experience stories). The discourse of CRT acknowledges an interactive relationship between the researcher and participants (Guba and Lincoln 1994) as well as
between the participants and their stories. Within this worldview, people's stories
of their experiences are counted as empirical evidence, as fact. Stories, experiences, and voices are the media through which we interpret reality. Critical race
theorists argue that only by looking at the stories and having access to the "experi-
ential knowledge" of those who have been victimized by racial inequities can we
understand the "socially ingrained" and "systemic forces at work in their oppression" (Pizarro 1998, 62).

Narrative Part 1

In elementary school, Frantz recalled socializing with the majority of his classmates. Living in a small community allowed him the opportunity to get to know his
classmates quite well from an early age. He recalled looking forward to the first
day of school each year to see if he would have the opportunity to make new
friends. During the course of the year, when it was time to work in teams, he would
work with the same group of friends repeatedly. As he got older, the first day of
school was always bittersweet due to the fact that with each passing year some of

his friends from previous years would be assigned to other classes; however, he viewed this as an opportunity to make new friends and to get to know more people.

By the time he reached fifth grade, he noticed that most of his peers had been with him since the third grade. He never gave it much thought other than the fact that he got closer with the friends he saw every day. Besides, he could still see his old friends during recess, after lunch.

As Frantz graduated to middle school, he wondered if multiple classes would mean that he might have his friends from early elementary school in some of his classes. He was amazed to see that the majority of his classes encompassed many of his classmates from the fourth and fifth grades. The rest of his classmates were students from other elementary schools. None of his friends from the early years were in any of his classes. Nonetheless, Frantz looked forward to lunchtime to catch up with his lost friends.

Narrative Part 2

As Frantz entered his second year of middle school, he began to wonder why he had the same core of classmates. One morning, while pondering this experience, he saw one of his former White classmates, Paul, a familiar face from his elementary school who hadn't been in any of his classes for years, even though they were in the same grade. After engaging Paul in the usual middle school small talk, Frantz began talking about his schedule.

Frantz asserted, "I'm really excited about my classes this year. My counselor, Mr. Smith (a Caucasian, middle-aged individual), helped me to sign up for classes. He's so cool because he wanted to make sure that I didn't sign up for anything that would be too hard for me. He even warned me that one of the toughest classes I will take this year is Foundations in Mathematics. He wanted to make sure that the rest of my classes would not be so hard that I couldn't concentrate on getting through this one. So what about you? What classes are you taking this semester?"

"Foundations of Mathematics? I'm taking pre-algebra! " Paul responded. "Mr. Smith told me that this class as well as other classes I'm taking would be a challenge, but if I stuck with it, after this year, I can take Algebra One and Physical Science in eighth grade for high school credit."

Frantz, puzzled, said, "I never knew that you could get high school credit in middle school. I wonder why Mr. Smith never told me about that. I'll ask him if I can take any of those classes that offer high school credit."

Later that afternoon, Frantz shared the conversation with Mr. Smith. Mr. Smith told Frantz that only a few courses offer high school credit, and he did not think Frantz could handle the extremely difficult classes Paul was preparing to take. Franz found the response overwhelming and could not respond to Mr. Smith.

Mr. Smith added, "You're doing fine with your current course load, aren't you? If you try to follow Paul, you risk flunking out of school! Trust me, stick to our plan, and things will be fine."

After this meeting, Frantz didn't know how to feel about things. He questioned why he had not received the same advice as Paul. What was so unique about Paul that afforded him these special opportunities? "Would I ever have found out about the availability of high school credit in middle school if Paul had not mentioned it?" Frantz wondered. He began asking his friends about their schedules and advice they received from counselors. To his surprise, very few of his Black friends knew about this option; most of them had been advised to pursue the same schedule as Frantz. However, many of his former White classmates were aware and were enrolled in these classes. Frantz wondered, "What is it we're missing or don't have that causes the counselors to think that we can't handle the advanced classes?"

Confused and upset, Frantz talked with his parents. After listening to the troubling account from their son, Frantz's parents arranged a conference with his counselor, Mr. Smith, the school principal, and Frantz. During this meeting, Mr. Smith maintained that he had developed the best academic route for Frantz. Frantz's parents adamantly expressed their concern over the low expectations being imposed on their son by his counselor. After debating back and forth, the principal suggested a compromise: that Frantz be allowed to sign up for a few prep courses as an eighth grader to prepare him for a more academic route as a freshman in high school. At the time, this suggestion seemed to satisfy all parties. Although Frantz never became a straight-A student, for the next year and a half, he worked hard in his classes to prepare for high school. Frantz felt that he had a lot to prove to those individuals who did not believe in his academic abilities. He was determined that, given the opportunity to excel, he would not waste it.

Narrative Part 3

After completing eighth grade, Frantz envisioned high school as an opportunity to leave his past behind and prove that he was as academically capable as any other student. Frantz and his family frequently discussed their hopes for him to become the first in the family to attend college.

As Frantz began his first semester, one of the classes that intrigued him was "Introduction to U.S. History." His interest in history had been nurtured over the years at family gatherings as he heard relatives talk about their experiences. His older uncles talked often of fighting for their country in Vietnam. Other relatives told stories of their experiences during the second world war. Frantz listened intently and gained a wealth of knowledge about contemporary history. He was excited that his history class would give him an opportunity to impress his teacher by sharing what he had learned outside of school. This class would prove to be pivotal, just not in the way Frantz had hoped.

The history class became a constant battle in verbal jousting between Frantz and his teacher, Mrs. Swank. Mrs. Swank was a White woman who had taught U.S. history for over thirty years in the high school. The class consisted of three Black students (Frantz included), two Latino students, and twenty-two White students. As the class began, Frantz was disturbed to find that the textbook had little, if anything, to say about the contributions of Blacks in U.S. history. Frantz waited in vain the first few weeks of school for an opening to discuss the experiences of his uncles. As he looked ahead in the textbook, he did not see any opportunities in sight. This, coupled with his teacher's approach to romanticizing U.S. history, bothered Frantz.

During the second month of school, Frantz's frustration led him to confront Mrs. Swank about his concerns one day as class began. Mrs. Swank explained that during the month of February several of the achievements of Blacks would be highlighted, and she moved on with her planned lesson. Frantz began to get upset because he did not feel that his history was being respected, and he felt that as an American, his story was just as important as anyone else's in the room. He interrupted Mrs. Swank and shared that this was not satisfactory in his opinion: "You make it sound like our contributions to this country are so limited that they can be summed up in thirty days or less! I know my uncles, as well as other Blacks, risked their lives for this country time and time again, but there is no mention of their role in this book. I think something is definitely wrong with this class!" Mrs. Swank responded, "If you value the opportunity to learn in this classroom, you will calm yourself and stop interrupting me!" Frantz countered, "Don't you think that my history is as important as yours?" Mrs. Swank warned, "That's enough! One more word and you're out of here!" Frantz exploded, "Forget this class! You're just teaching a bunch of racist jibber-jabber anyway!"

This exchange resulted in Frantz not only being sent to the office for disrupting the class and insubordination but also in a suspension from school. Even worse, he developed an early reputation as a troublemaker, with this being the first of several referrals and suspensions he would receive during his freshman year. Frantz's grades declined as his attitude toward school soured. He found himself losing interest in his classes and looking at possible electives and vocational courses for the following year. His dreams of college were rapidly disappearing as he wondered, "What's the point anyway?"

The following year, Frantz had to repeat the U.S. history course. This time around, however, he decided to take the course with Mrs. Daniels, an African American woman in her second year of teaching. Being relatively new to teaching, Mrs. Daniels was part of a mentoring program to support new teachers. Unbeknownst to Frantz, Mrs. Daniels's mentor was Mrs. Swank (the department chair). However, Frantz as well as his family hoped that this teacher would provide an improved experience for him that would perhaps get him back on track academically.

Early in the first quarter of the academic year, Frantz was disappointed to notice that Mrs. Daniels was teaching the curriculum in the same manner Mrs. Swank used to. Following the advice of her mentor, she would follow the textbook step by step to ensure that she covered what the students needed to know in this course. Recognizing the developing pattern, Frantz's family made a request that Frantz be transferred to Mr. Newbold's class at the beginning of the second quarter. Mr. Newbold was an African American, seasoned teacher with a reputation for turning "problem kids" around.

With Frantz repeating the course, Mr. Newbold reviewed his records for the past year. He also spoke to Mrs. Swank, Mrs. Daniels, Frantz's family, and Frantz to gain their perspectives on how to help Frantz turn things around. Mrs. Swank exclaimed, "He has little if any understanding of academic discipline, he constantly challenges authority, and to top it off, he had the nerve to call me a racist!" Mrs. Daniels expressed her frustration in being overwhelmed by trying to find her way as a new teacher. She did not feel as if she had the time to extend the current curriculum. As a result, she leaned heavily on the advice of Mrs. Swank to follow the textbook. After all, this way she would be certain that she covered the majority, if not all, of the needed curriculum to prepare the students for part 2 of U.S. History. Frantz and his family explained to Mr. Newbold their perception that Frantz's attempted contributions to class discussions were not valued. They believed wholeheartedly that, if given the chance to redeem himself, Frantz could flourish in the classroom. Mr. Newbold also was convinced that it was not too late for Frantz.

As the course began, Frantz was delighted in the change of atmosphere in the classroom. Mr. Newbold used the textbook as a springboard that led to critical discussions in class about the information. The renowned phrase in his class was "Whose perspective is this text coming from, and what information did they possibly omit?" Frantz thrived under Mr. Newbold's approach and found himself contributing daily to class discussions. Mr. Newbold also spent time after school with Frantz to talk about the importance of not allowing others to get in the way of what he wants and needs to accomplish.

Frantz gravitated to his new teacher and opened up to him. He expressed his frustration with having been labeled a troublemaker within the school, which had led to teachers waiting to "catch him doing something wrong." Frantz questioned what the future held for him. His family's experiences led him to hold out little hope. He related, "My uncles talked about the fact that they volunteered to fight in Vietnam, and when they returned home, they still were treated as though they were inferior to Whites—uniform or no uniform! The same thing is happening to me! I wish there was something I could do to change everything." Mr. Newbold acknowledged that racism and bigotry have been an inherent part of the United States since its inception, but he offered hope. He added, "I truly believe that although things aren't the way they should be, they are progressively getting better. Opportunities that did not exist for African Americans when I was your age are now made obtainable. The only way we can rise above injustices is through excellence. Dropping out of school will not provide you with the tools to fight for equality and justice for all. This is why you must work hard to make sure that you prepare yourself intellectually so that you can do something to change things." With Mr. Newbold's support, Frantz not only flourished in his history class but in all other courses as he set his sights on college.

Aftermath of the *Brown* Decision

Nearly fifty years following the landmark *Brown* case, many of the points argued by Thurgood Marshall have yet to reach fruition. Consequently, current conditions warrant a re-examination of the alleged benefits of *Brown*.

The central question addressed by the Supreme Court in the *Brown* cases was whether segregation of children in public schools solely on the basis of race deprives minority children of equal educational opportunities even when all else is equal. The court ruled that not only was such racial segregation harmful, but also that to separate Black children from others of similar age and qualifications solely because of their race generates a feeling of inferiority as to their status in the community that may affect their hearts and minds in a way unlikely ever to be undone. The courts asserted that the need for African American children to see themselves in a positive reaffirming way was just as important as curricula, facilities, and other resources.

The question with which the justices wrestled represents a long-standing quest for educational equality for Blacks. Howe (1997), within a liberal framework, asserted that the problem underlying this issue surrounds a lack of political understanding of what equality of educational opportunity requires. In support of this claim, James Coleman (1968) observed that the concept of equality of educational opportunity has a variety of interpretations. As a result, empirical data can be interpreted in a multitude of ways, which can lead to numerous meanings with varied implications for educational policy. This phenomenon presents problems for a court in weighing conflicting ideas with respect to what it means to treat people equally.

In 1955, the Supreme Court determined that segregation should be ended as soon as possible, but the court also recognized that it would be difficult for communities to deal with the change and that there were many institutional, political, and social circumstances to be worked out. The court struggled with how to phrase the order to desegregate schools and what kind of timeframes should be attached to implementing the order. The National Association for the Advancement of Colored People advocated for schools to be desegregated "forthwith," which implies a quick timetable. However, Justice Warren adopted the advice of Justice Frankfurter and chose other language. After hearing further arguments on implementation, the court declared in

1955 that schools must be desegregated with "all deliberate speed." Delivering the unanimous majority opinion, Justice Warren stated:

> Full implementation of these constitutional principles may require solution of varied local school problems. School authorities have the primary responsibility for elucidating, assessing, and solving these problems; courts will have to consider whether the action of school authorities constitutes good faith implementation of the governing constitutional principles. (Brown v. Board 1955, 299)

Over the past fifty years, we have seen a plethora of laws, programs, and approaches to accomplish the court order. The shortcoming of the legal remedy is glaringly evident; laws cannot legislate the thinking and core beliefs of those it governs.

After being forced to integrate, many White communities withdrew support for public schools and established private academies. These schools were primarily targeted at European American parents and were sometimes supported with public funds. White private academies flourished with state-supported tuition (White 1994).

Desegregation was achieved mostly by closing schools serving African American students and busing the students to former Whites-only schools. Busing students was never popular among White parents. Today, many African American parents also express unwillingness to have their children bused, or their neighborhood school closed, to achieve racial balance. Many Black parents believe their children are better off in resegregated schools because they no longer believe desegregated schools offer any significant academic advantage. This belief among some Black parents may be a response to the resegregation that often occurs within schools via course assignments and "ability grouping," as demonstrated in the first two parts of the narrative presented in this article. A pattern develops in which mostly low-income Black students experience initial learning difficulties in the early grades, then are evaluated as being of low ability and placed in low-track, remedial, or special education programs. When they enter high school, they are enrolled primarily in vocational and general programs, while Whites and many students of high socioeconomic status are enrolled in academic programs (Oakes 1990).

Some observers see the persistent segregation of African Americans, whether through private schooling, resistance to busing, or tracking, as a result of African American parents' lack of ability to mobilize power and resources (Lipman 1997). Decision-making structures limit the influence of African American parents (especially those with low incomes) can have on educational decisions affecting their children. They have few avenues by which they can challenge curriculum choices, instructional strategies, or course placement decisions. As demonstrated in the third narrative, school officials often dismiss African American students' absence in advanced and college preparatory courses as a normal reflection of the students' interests, academic talents, and/or parents' lack of interest. However, African American parents have long cared deeply about education, and so have their children (Billingsley 1992). Besides the ongoing effects of segregation, a number of other factors affect educational outcomes for rural and urban African Americans.

National data indicate that African American and Hispanic American students, as subpopulations, still do not score as well as their European American counterparts. A recent study by the Western Interstate Commission for Higher Education (1998) found that students in rural, small town locations in southern states such as Alabama, Arkansas, Delaware, Florida, Georgia, Kentucky, Louisiana, Maryland, Mississippi, Oklahoma, South Carolina, Tennessee, Texas, Virginia, and West Virginia, score significantly below students in other rural areas nationwide. Moreover, rural schools in all states have less money and poorer educational programs than their more wealthy urban neighbors (Alexander 1990).

Mr. Newbold in the third narrative demonstrated that for many African American children, African American teachers represent surrogate parent figures, acting as disciplinarians, counselors, role models, and advocates. According to one study, low-achieving African American students benefit most from relationships with African American teachers (King 1993). Yet, with integration significant numbers of African American teachers lost their positions: Between 1954 and 1965, thirty-eight thousand African Americans in seventeen states lost their positions as teachers and administrators (Holmes 1990, King 1993). As recently as the 1995–1996 school year, African American teachers comprised only 7.3 percent of the teaching force in public schools (National Education Association 1997). It is important to note that the solution to improving the academic performance of African American students cannot be achieved by simply providing them with African American teachers. Teachers who graduate from teacher preparation programs (including African Americans) are products of the system who have been trained to reproduce the results the system has produced. Woodson (1933) described the uncritically educated African American as follows:

> For the arduous task of serving (their) race … the Negro graduate has little or no training at all. The people whom he has been ordered to serve have been belittled by his teachers to the extent that he can hardly find delight in undertaking what his education has led him to think is impossible. Considering his race as blank in achievement, then, he sets out to stimulate their imitation of others. The performance is kept up a while; but, like any other effort at meaningless imitation, it results in failure. (6)

Teachers need to be adequately prepared to meet the needs of marginalized students. This point was demonstrated by varied levels of success Frantz experienced under Mrs. Daniels and Mr. Newbold. Whereas Mrs. Daniels may have genuinely wanted to do a good job teaching her students, her approach resulted from her teacher preparation and uncritical acceptance of the outcomes that result.

Part 3 of the narrative shows that resistance to school norms is also a factor with African American students. Instead of submitting to the norms of a school establishment many students experience as oppressive, some students reject European American speech patterns and devalue high academic achievement, inadvertently limiting themselves (Fordham and Ogbu 1986, King 1993, Ogbu 1990). However, not all Black students respond in this manner. High-achieving African American students refer to their awareness of racism and prejudice as a reason to excel, thus preparing themselves to fight these evils (King 1993, Sanders 1997).

Conclusion

I surmise that Dr. Carter G. Woodson understood long ago that it would be fruitless to examine the progress of African Americans within public schools solely in its contemporary context. Unfortunately, this mistake is made daily in public schools. The abysmal failure of many African American students within public schools is oftentimes explained, rationalized, and dismissed as a product of today's disinterested parents, lazy students, and media influence—none of which look at the historical structures (e.g., schooling) that influence contemporary culture. Therefore, I used CRT in this article to show that biases in public schools are institutionalized, systemic, and cumulative. CRT also illuminates the glaring shortcomings of liberal attempts to provide equal educational opportunities. Western civilization is built around liberalism, which results in reproducing inequity, not creating impartial situations for the nondominant races (Goldberg 1993).

CRT also sheds light on the fact that these outputs are often supported and forwarded through structures that permeate society, such as law. For example, one of the alleged benefits of *Brown* was to ensure that Black children would have equal access to the resources of their White counterparts. Frantz's story painfully portrays practices that continue to deny African American students equal educational opportunity. Contemporary attempts to rectify the glaring inequities that exist in education, such as the No Child Left Behind legislation, still cause me to question whether America truly wants to educate all of its children. In moving from theory to practice, I believe that public schools have enormous potential to liberating those individuals (African Americans in particular) on the margins. The tragedy of this matter is that this potential has remained untapped. Although pockets of resistance strive to reverse this trend, for the most part, schooling in America still marginalizes minority groups.

Contemporary efforts that focus on "fixing" the students will provide only short-term relief of these issues. If the United States truly hopes to "leave no child behind," then we need to literally dismantle and reconstruct systemic approaches currently in place within the educational system. This will require a full-fledged commitment on behalf of all stakeholders to confront difficult questions such as the following:

1. What type of preparation is needed for future teachers entering the field?
2. Do laws (or problematic interpretation of laws) perpetuate inequities?
3. What changes are needed to current curricula to provide a more liberating effect for all students (those marginalized as well as those who are members of the dominant society)?
4. What systemic structures in school and society contain racist underpinnings?

It is time to move away from the continuous mis- and de-educating that has historically occurred within public schools and move toward generating spaces where praxis amongst all stakeholders is embraced.

Notes

1. Here I am leaning on positions forwarded by Charles Mills (1998) in *Blackness Visible: Essays on Philosophy and Race.*
2. These are excerpts from a PowerPoint presentation entitled "African American Achievement in America," created by the Education Trust Inc. (2003). Available online at http://www2.edtrust.org/EdTrust/Press+Room/2004+reports.htm
3. These statistics are taken from a PowerPoint presentation entitled "African American Achievement in America," created by the Education Trust Inc. (2003). Available online at http://www2.edtrust.org/EdTrust/Press+Room/2004+reports.htm

References

Alexander, K. 1990. "Rural Education: Institutionalization of Disadvantage." *Journal of Education Finance*, 16:121.

Atkinson, Pansye and Fred Hord. 1983. *Save the Children.* Frostbury: Office of Minority Affairs.

Bennett, Lerone. 1972. Excerpts from "The Challenge of Blackness," delivered by Lerone Bennett at the Institute of the Black World in Atlanta, Georgia.

Billingsley, Andrew. 1992. *Climbing Jacob's Ladder: The Enduring Legacy of African American Families.* New York: Simon &Schuster.

Brown v. Board of Education of Topeka, Kansas, 347 U.S. 483 (1954).

Brown v. Board of Education of Topeka, Kansas, 349 U.S. 294 (1955).

Carnegie Corporation of New York. 1984/1985. "Renegotiating Society's Contract With the Public Schools." *Carnegie Quarterly* 29/30:1–4, 6–11.

Coleman, J. 1968. "The Concept of Equality of Educational Opportunity." *Harvard Educational Review*, 38 (1):7–22.

College Board. 1985. *Equality and Excellence: The Educational Status of Black Americans.* New York: Author.

Delgado, Richard. 1995. *Critical Race Theory: The Cutting Edge.* Philadelphia, Penn.: Temple University Press.

Dubois, W. E. B. 1973. *The Education of Black People: Ten Critiques 1906–1960.* Amherst: University of Massachusetts Press.

Education Trust, Inc. 2004. *African American Achievement in America, 2003.* Available online at http://www2.edtrust.org/EdTrust/Press+Room/2004+reports.htm

Fordham, Signithia, and John U. Ogbu. 1986. "Black Students' School Success: Coping With the "Burden of 'Acting White.'" *Urban Review* 18:176–206.

Goldberg, David T. 1993. *Racist Culture: Philosophy and the Politics of Meaning.* Cambridge, Mass: Blackwell.

Guba, E. G., and Y. S. Lincoln. 1994. "Competing Paradigms in Qualitative Research." In *Handbook of Qualitative Research,* edited by N. K. Denzin and Y. S. Lincoln. Thousand Oaks, Calif: SAGE Publications.

Hale, Janice E. 1986. *Black Children: Their Roots, Culture, and Learning Styles.* Baltimore: John Hopkins University Press.

Holmes, B. J. 1990. "New Strategies Are Needed to Produce Minority Teachers," In *Recruiting and Retaining Minority Teachers*, Policy Brief No. 8, edited by A. Dorman. Oak Brook, Ill.: North Central Regional Educational Laboratory.

Howe, Kenneth. 1997. *Understanding Equal Educational Opportunity: Social Justice, Democracy, and Schooling,* New York: Teachers College Press.

King, Sabrina Hope. 1993. "The Limited Presence of African-American Teachers." *Review of Educational Research* 63:115–149.

Kowalski, Theodore J., and Ulrich C. Reitzug. 1993. *Contemporary School Administration: An Introduction.* New York: Longman.

Ladson-Billings, Gloria. 1999. "Just What Is Critical Race Theory, and What's it Doing in a Nice Field Like Education?" In *Race Is ... Race Isn't*, edited by L. Parker, D. Deyhl, and Sofia Villenas, 7–30. Boulder, Col.: Westview Press.

Lipman, Pauline. 1997. "Restructuring in Context: A Case Study of Teacher Participation and the Dynamics of Ideology, Race, and Power." *American Educational Research Review* 34:3–37.

Mills, Charles. 1998. *Blackness Visible: Essays on Philosophy and Race.* Ithaca, N.Y.: Cornell University Press.

National Education Association. 1997. *Survey of State Legislation Affecting Teacher and Educational Support Personnel Retirement.* Washington, D.C.: National Education Association.

Oakes, Jeannie. 1990. *Multiplying Inequities: The Effects of Race, Social Class, and Tracking on Opportunities to Learn Mathematics and Science.* Santa Monica, Calif.: Rand Corporation.

Ogbu, John U. 1990. Literacy and Schooling in Subordinate Cultures: The Case of Black Americans. In *Going to School: The African American Experience,* edited by K. Lomotey, 113–181. Albany: State University of New York Press.

Pizarro, M. 1998. "Chicana/o Power! Epistemology and Methodology for Social Justice and Empowerment in Chicana/o Communities." *Qualitative Studies in Education*, 11 (1):57–80.

Sanders, M. G. 1997. "*Overcoming Obstacles: Academic Achievement as a Response to Racism and Discrimination.*" *Journal of Negro Education* 66 (1) 83.

Tate, W. F. 1996. "*Critical Race Theory.*" *Review of Research in Education* 22:201–247.

Western Interstate Commission for Higher Education. 1998. *Knocking at the College Door: Projections of High School Graduates by State and Race/Ethnicity 1996–2012.*

White, Forrest R. 1994. "Brown Revisited." *Phi Delta Kappan* 76:12–20.

Woodson, Carter G. 1933. *The Mis-Education of the Negro.* Trenton, N.J.: First Africa World Press, Inc.

Correspondence should be addressed to Craig A. Saddler, 111 Melanee Lane, Oxford, OH 45056. E-mail: saddleca@muohio.edu

Legal Challenges to Segregated Education in Topeka, Kansas, 1903–1941

JAMIE B. LEWIS
University of Georgia–Athens

This article provides a brief overview of segregated education in Kansas and then explores 3 legal cases: (a) *Reynolds v. The Board of Education of the City of Topeka* (1903), (b) *Wright v. Board of Education of Topeka* (1930), and (c) *Graham v. Board of Education of Topeka* (1941), the precursors to *Brown v. Board of Education of Topeka, Kansas* (1954). These lawsuits, brought by Black citizens in Topeka, Kansas, provide insights into the legal challenges to segregated education in Topeka prior to Brown and provide an analysis of the legal role Topeka played in terms of shaping and influencing the terrain of segregated education in not only Kansas but the United States.

In mid-September 1953, Charles S. Scott, an attorney in Topeka, Kansas, received a Western Union telegram from Thurgood Marshall stating: "Have just received information on latest action. Topeka School Board completely abolishing all segregation this year. Please advise."[1] Marshall's telegram was sent not as a congratulatory measure or as an act of elation due to a victory against segregated education; instead, it was sent out of concern about the setback this action could potentially have with regard to the legal campaign being waged against segregated education. The Topeka school board's action caused concern for Marshall and the members of the legal team of the National Association for the Advancement of Colored People (NAACP) because it could have resulted in the U.S. Supreme Court refusing to hear arguments in the appeal of the Kansas case because the issue had become moot.

Of the five cases involved in what has become known collectively as *Brown v. Board of Education of Topeka, Kansas* (1954), the Kansas case was unique. According to Paul Wilson, the assistant state attorney who represented Kansas:

> among the state cases, only in Topeka was there a finding of no substantial inequality. Only in the Kansas case was the record not cluttered with issues of the inferiority of the Negro schools. If Brown had not been on the Supreme Court's docket, a decision favoring the plaintiffs might have been based on inequality, and the constitutionality of segregation *per se* left undetermined. (Wilson 1995, 21)

Its uniqueness on the national level is somewhat paradoxical because the legal issue at the state level in Kansas had centered around equality. At the state level, its uniqueness is derived from the fact that the legal focus shifted toward segregation. In this regard, the *Brown* case represented a shift away from concerns about equal educational opportunities. In addition to the role it played in *Brown*, Topeka provides an interesting site through which to examine and contextualize the issues surrounding segregated education, because *Brown* marked the culmination of fifty years of legal advocacy against segregated education in Topeka.[2] In this article I provide a brief overview of segregated education in Kansas, then explore the three legal cases brought by Black citizens in Topeka prior to *Brown* and provide an analysis of the legal role Topeka played in terms of shaping and influencing the terrain of segregated education not only in Kansas but the entire United States.

Segregated Education in Kansas

The first education law governing the Kansas territory, passed in July 1855, provided for the creation, governance, and financing of "a system of district schools that should be free and open to every class of white citizens of appropriate age" (Wilson 1995, 33). In 1858, after the Free State Party gained control of the territorial legislature, the school code was revised and the word *white* was eliminated. When admitted to statehood on January 29, 1861, the Kansas Constitution provided that "the legislature should establish a uniform system of public schools and schools of higher grade" (Wilson 1995, 32).

When the state legislature convened in March 1861, a body of school laws was enacted. These laws provided for the establishment of a system of common schools and permitted segregated education. The language of this law is interesting because the separation of White and Black children was not mandated. The statute allowed the local school boards to determine whether education should be segregated. The law also created an obligation to secure "equal education advantages" (Wilson 1995, 36) to White and Black children. Separate education was permissible as long as it was equal.

In 1868 (after the Civil War and the passage of the 13th and 14th Amendments), the Kansas legislature enacted a general statute that created first-class and second-class cities. *First-class cities* had populations of fifteen thousand or more, and *second-class cities* had populations of more than two thousand and less than fifteen thousand. This legislation permitted first-class cities "to organize and maintain racially separate schools." At the time, Leavenworth, which had been a stronghold for pro-slavery advocates during territorial times, was the only city in Kansas large enough to qualify as a first-class city. Second-class cities were not allowed to operate segregated schools. An "act for the regulation and support of common schools" was passed in 1875. This enactment repealed all existing school laws and did not contain any provisions regarding the segregation of schoolchildren on the basis of race.

In 1879, the migration of formerly enslaved Africans led to an increase in the African American population in Kansas, particularly in urban areas. Commonly referred to as the *Exodus*, this migration is considered to be the first major Black migration from the South. These *Exodusters* came primarily from Tennessee, Alabama, and Mississippi (Painter [1976] 1986). In Topeka, the migration of the Exodusters resulted in a 404 percent increase in Topeka's Black population. "By 1880, Black Topekans numbered 3,648 in a total population of 15,528" (Cox 1982, 42). The Exodusters resided in areas that came to be known as "Tennessee Town" and "the Bottoms. " That same year, the Kansas legislature amended the 1868 school code and, with regard to first-class cities, provided that "the board of education shall have power ... to organize and maintain separate schools for the education of white and colored children, except in high school, where no discrimination shall be made on account of color." There were only three cities in Kansas that qualified as first-class cities during this time: Leavenworth, Atchison, and Topeka. The segregated-education law was permissive in that segregation was not required; local school districts could choose to segregate schools on the basis of race. The law was also restrictive in that it allowed only cities of a certain size to segregate education by race.[3]

Legal Resistance to Segregated Education

Kansas has a rich legal history with regard to segregated education. Between 1881 and 1951, twelve legal cases challenging segregated education were brought into the purview of the judicial system. The Kansas Supreme Court decided eleven cases; the remaining decision was *Brown*, which was filed in the federal court system. The three cases discussed in this article—*Reynolds v. The Board of Education of the City of Topeka* (1903), *Wright v. Board of Education of Topeka,* (1930), and *Graham v. Board of Education of Topeka*, (1941)—were the precursors to *Brown* and provide insights into segregated education in Topeka. Black protest activities in Topeka began as early as 1873, with churches serving as the primary institutions through which organized efforts to effectuate race progress and to address racial discrimination were developed. Additionally, during this time, a number of fraternal organizations were established, and these were also used as forums to address inequities (Cox 1982, 29–33).

Reynolds v. The Board of Education of the City of Topeka (1903)

During 1890, Lowman Hill was annexed into the City of Topeka. At the time of the annexation, children residing in Lowman Hill went to the same school, irrespective of their race. Although Topeka had established separate schools prior to 1890 throughout the city, it lacked sufficient financial resources to maintain two schools in Lowman Hills. After the school building was destroyed by fire on July

20, 1900, the school district selected a location, and construction began on a new "first class modern school building" (Brief of Defendant, Kansas State Supreme Court Records, *Reynolds v. Board of Education of Topeka* [hereinafter Reynolds, *Brief of Defendant 1903*]). The Black community was led to believe the school was being built for all of the children residing in the Lowman Hill area. According to William Reynolds, after the White community circulated a petition requesting the establishment of separate schools, the Black community sent a committee to the superintendent requesting to see the petition. They were assured that the school district was building only one school and that it would be open to both races.

In spite of these assurances, on February 2, 1902, an article entitled "A Place for Niggers" was published in the Topeka *Journal*, which discussed the establishment of a separate school for the Black children in the Lowman Hills area. The school district had moved a building to the old school site and fixed it up for use as the Black school. Instead of reporting to Douglas, the Black school, on the first Monday in February 1902, William Reynolds took his son, Raoul, to Lowman Hills, the new White school building. He was denied admission and protested sending his son to Douglas because of its unsanitary conditions. The Black community contended that the Douglas school was unfit, because after the fire the basement of the old school had been used not only to dump rubbish but also as a place for the streetcar workers to relieve themselves. The Black community was also concerned about the stench created by flooding in times of heavy rain. The culvert used to carry off sewage and excess water was located across from the school.

The school board asserted that "the Board made no secret of the fact that [the site] was purchased for a white school" (*Reynolds*, Brief of Defendant 1903, 90, 139). Separate schools were established "for the reason that the colored pupils—especially in their initial years—need a little different discipline from the white pupils, have somewhat different intellectual requirements, and for the reason that in mixed schools quarrels are frequent between the two races" (*Reynolds*, Brief of Defendant 1903, 2). Additionally, the board asserted the assignment of the White children to the new school building was based on the number of children in the school district rather than their race. Because there were 175 White children and 35 Black children, the larger building was used for the White children. The school district identified several White schools—Jackson, Grant, and Quincy—that were older than the Black school. The school district stated that Lowman Hills was more centrally located to the residences of the White children and Douglas was more centrally located to the residences of the Black children. The furnishings of both schools were similar. The school board argued that the furnishings in the Douglas school building were in better condition because the Lowman Hill furniture had been damaged by the fire in the temporary Campbell Court facility.

The school district denied that the site was unfit and provided evidence of the use of the well water by local residents. The school district supported this testimony with that of an engineer who had tested the water and found it to be safe.

Thomas Lloyd, the janitor, and two men who worked on the building after it had been moved, testified that the basement area had been properly cleaned. The school district also denied that water stood in front of the school as deeply as was asserted by the plaintiffs.

The Kansas Supreme Court addressed three legal challenges to segregated education. First, Gaspar C. Clemons and F. J. Lynch, the attorneys representing the Reynolds, argued section 6290 of the Kansas General Statutes of 1901, which provided that "the Board of Education shall have power to organize and maintain separate schools for the education of white and colored children" (Brief of Plaintiff, Kansas State Supreme Court Records, *Reynolds v. Board of Education of Topeka*, 1903 [hereinafter Reynolds, *Brief of Plaintiff 1903*]) violated section 2, article 6, of the Kansas State Constitution that required the establishment of a uniform system of common schools. Clemons and Lynch argued that segregated schools were not common and that Kansas's bifurcated system of segregation was not uniform (*Reynolds*, Brief of Defendant 1903, 30). They argued that "*every* school was to be a 'common' school. *No* school was to be a *select* or class school" (Reynolds, Brief of Plaintiff 1903, 8). This argument paralleled Justice Valentine's judgment in *Tinnon,* where he stated that if the school district provided one school for Black children then it was not maintaining "common schools free to all children of the city" (*Board of Education of Ottawa v. Tinnon*, 1881). Clemens and Lynch urged the court to adopt "one inflexible definition of the term 'common schools.' [They believed] there must be one and the same meaning for all constitutional purposes" (Reynolds, Brief of Plaintiff 1903, 11).

Clemens and Lynch next argued that the bifurcated system of segregated schools in Kansas was not uniform; a uniform system was one that was the same throughout the state. They asked:

> Can any reason be given why the five cities of the first class should have power to establish and maintain separate schools for white and colored children when that power is denied, not only to every other rural district, but to all other cities of the state? Are the white children whiter or the colored children blacker in Leavenworth, than in Ottawa? (Reynolds, Brief of Plaintiff 1903, 13)

Clemens and Lynch argued that if Kansas was "to have separate schools, let there be a statute establishing 'a uniform system' of separate schools. If segregation be lawful at all, it must be uniform and systematic"(Reynolds, Brief of Plaintiff 1903, 13). Because two systems existed, one permitting segregated schools and one prohibiting segregated schools, Clemens and Lynch urged the court to find that the statute governing first-class cities violated the Kansas Constitution's requirement that education in the state be a common and uniform system.

Their second argument contended that segregated education violated the 14th Amendment of the U.S. Constitution. They provided two grounds on which the

14th Amendment was violated. The first reason was that the guarantee of the equal protection of the laws was violated by the exclusion of the Black children from "common" schools on the basis of race. Although they acknowledged that the majority decision in *Plessy v. Ferguson* (1896) opened the door for segregated schools, they urged the Kansas court to heed the words of Justice Harlan and invalidate the education law legalizing "the drawing of 'the color line'" (Reynolds, Brief of Plaintiff 1903, 16). The second rationale provided for finding a violation of the 14th Amendment was that even if separate schools were permissible, the statute was void because it did not require school boards to provide equal facilities. Clemens and Lynch proposed that because the Kansas law lacked a mandate for equality, school boards "may build an educational palace for the whites and give the colored children hovel without violating" the statute (Reynolds, Brief of Plaintiff 1903, 17). They argued that this is what happened in Topeka when the board built a new first-class modern building for the White children and refurbished an older school building for the Black children.

The final issue presented by Clemens and Lynch challenged the validity of the 1879 Kansas education statute because it attempted to amend a law that had been repealed. If *Reynolds* succeeded in invalidating the 1879 act, then the valid law would have been the 1875 statute that repealed all existing school laws and did not contain any provisions allowing for the segregation of schoolchildren on the basis of race. Therefore, first-class cities would have lacked the authority to segregate schools.

The Topeka Board of Education, represented by J. H. Gleed and John L. Hunt, argued that the 14th Amendment was not applicable because public education was a privilege and immunity of state citizenship, and the right to establish separate schools for Blacks and Whites had been recognized by the U.S. Supreme Court as a valid exercise of state authority. They argued:

> Equality of right does not involve the necessity of educating children of both sexes, or children without regard to their attainments or age, in the same school. Any classification which preserves substantially equal school advantages does not impair any rights, and is not prohibited by the Constitution of the United States. Equality of rights does not necessarily imply identity of rights. (*Reynolds*, Brief of Defendant 1903, 23)

They stated that the provision of equal school advantages did not require that children be educated in the same schools; instead, it allowed for the classification of students as long as substantially equal school advantages were provided.

Gleed and Hunt countered Reynolds's position that separate schools for Black and White children were not common and uniform by arguing that school boards must have the right to classify students:

> They may be classified with reference to their knowledge; they may be classi-
> fied territorially; they may be classified with reference to their respective needs;
> they may be classified with respect to the discipline they require; they may be
> classified in order to promote harmony and prevent dissension. (*Reynolds*, Brief
> of Defendant 1903, 56)

Gleed and Hunt posited that classification on the basis of race was due to the fact
"that the younger colored children need a little different discipline from the white
children and a different application of that discipline [and] ... that when younger
children are mingled in the same classes they do not agree, and that quarrels ensue"
(*Reynolds*, Brief of Defendant 1903, 56). However, no evidence was presented in-
dicating that when the children in Lowman Hills attended a mixed school that
school officials encountered disciplinary problems.

In their argument in support of the validity of the 1879 education statute, Gleed
and Hunt traced the pertinent educational enactments. The 1868 law contained an
express grant of authority to operate separate schools (Supplemental Brief for Defendant, *Reynolds v. Board of Education of Topeka* 1903 [hereinafter Reynolds,
Supplemental Brief for Defendant 1903]). They reasoned the law governing
first-class cities passed in 1874 expressly stated "this act shall not in any way
change or affect existing laws with reference to the public schools" (*Reynolds*,
Supplemental Brief for Defendant 1903, 2) and resulted in section 75 of the 1868
law, which remained the valid educational law. In 1876, the Kansas legislature enacted another law governing first-class cities. Section 4 of article 10 of this act gov-
erned education and provided that:

> The board of education shall have power to select their own officers; to make
> their rules and regulations subject to the provisions of this act; to establish a high
> school whenever in its opinion the educational interests of the city demand the
> same; and to exercise the sole control over the public schools and school prop-
> erty of the city. (*Reynolds*, Supplemental Brief for Defendant 1903, 3)

Gleed and Hunt argued this was a re-enactment, rather than a repeal, of "substantially all of the provisions of Article V in the Act of 1868" (*Reynolds*, Supplemental Brief for Defendant 1903, 2). Although the 1876 act does closely parallel the
1868 act, what was missing from this act was the clause expressly authorizing separate schools. However, Gleed and Hunt proposed that when the legislature passed
the 1879 legislation amending the 1868 education law, it was undertaking a valid
action. The 1879 legislation inserted the following language in section 75: "to organize and maintain separate schools for the education of white and colored children except in the high school, where no discrimination shall be made on account
of color" (*Reynolds*, Supplemental Brief for Defendant 1903, 3). The insertion of

this language gave school boards the power to segregate education, except at the high school level.

The opinion of the Kansas Supreme Court focused primarily on whether a valid legislative grant of authority to establish separate schools existed. The court determined that when the Kansas legislature passed the 1879 statute, they intended to reenact the 1868 statute granting first-class cities the power to operate separate schools. The court stated that the Kansas Constitution provided that repealed laws could be revived "if only the new enactment contain[ed] all revived matter, and [did] not merely make reference to it" (*Reynolds v. Board of Education of Topeka* 1903). Because the 1879 statute included the language from the 1868 act rather than referring to it, the mandates of the Kansas Constitution with regard to reviving a repealed law were satisfied. The court held that Topeka, as a first-class city, could operate separate schools for Black and White children.

The court then turned its attention to the argument that the provision of separate schools for Black and White children violated the Kansas Constitution's requirement of the establishment of a "uniform system of common schools" (*Reynolds v. Board of Education of Topeka* 1903, 277). The court determined that the term *common school* referred to a particular grade and rejected the definition proposed by Reynolds that *common* referred to schools that were "open to all." Adopting this definition of *common* was a departure from the position the court had taken in the *Tinnon* case, in which Justice Valentine had defined *common schools* as those that were open to all. Likewise, the court adopted the definition of *uniformity* accepted by the Indiana Supreme Court in *Cory v. Carter*: "Uniformity will be secured when all the schools of the same grade have the same system of government and discipline, the same branches of learning taught and the same qualifications for admission" (*Reynolds v. Board of Education of Topeka* 1903, 277). Therefore, the court found that a uniform system of common schools existed in Kansas and that the separation of children on the basis of race was a proper exercise of a school board's power to classify students. This position was also in opposition to the position the court had taken in the *Tinnon* line of precedent with regard to classifying students on the basis of race.

In addressing the issue of whether separate education violated the 14th Amendment, the Kansas Supreme Court relied on *Plessy*, as well as legal decisions from Ohio, New York, and California and announced that separate schools did not violate the U.S. Constitution. The final issue addressed by the court was whether the educational facilities provided to the Black children in the Douglas school were equal to those provided to the White children. The court found that no substantial discrimination had occurred. They stated that although it is

> true, for the accommodation of a numerous white population a much larger and more imposing school building is provided than that set apart for the few colored children in the district. This, however, is an incidental matter, and necessarily

unavoidable in the administration of any extended school system. Schoolhouses
cannot be identical in every respect; but parents cannot, on this account dictate
the one their children shall attend. (*Reynolds v. Board of Education of Topeka*
1903, 281)

The court relied on the New York case of *People ex. rel. King v. Gallagher* as authority for the position that what must be protected is equality of privileges and
rights, not identical privileges and rights.

Wright v. Board of Education of Topeka (1930)

George Wright sued the Board of Education of the City of Topeka in the district court of Shawnee County, requesting that the court issue an injunction allowing his daughter, Wilhemina, to continue attending Randolph school. The
Wrights lived in College Hill, an area two miles west of Washburn College that
had been annexed into the city of Topeka in 1925. At the time annexation was
sought, Mr. Duggins and Mr. Derby, trustees of the school district, approached
William Wright and asked him to sign a petition in support of the annexation.
According to Wright, Mr. Duggins "said they would have to have me. It would
take one more name, and if he could get me to sign the petition we would be in
the city for school purposes and they were going to build a new school" (Abstract of Record, *Wright v. Board of Education of Topeka* 1930 [hereinafter
Wright, *Abstract of Record*], 5). Initially, William Wright refused to sign the petition because of the impact it would have on the education of his children. Topeka was a first-class city and operated separate schools for Black and White
children. Because he lived outside the city limits, Mr. Williams's children attended the College Hill school with the White children.

The following Tuesday or Wednesday, Mr. Duggins brought the petition back to
Mr. Wright, assuring him that "the Board had authorized him to say that the old
settlers out in that neighborhood their children would continue to go there until
they graduated from school" (*Wright*, Abstract of Record 1930, 6). Relying on this
promise, Mr. Wright had his wife, Beatrice Wright, sign the petition because the
property was in her name.

Randolph, a new school, was built in 1926, and his children attended this
school. In November 1928, "Maude Rich presented her children for admission to
Randolph School" (Counter Abstract and Brief of Appellees, *Wright v. Board of
Education of Topeka* 1930 [hereinafter Wright, *Counter Abstract and Brief of Appellees*], 3). The principal denied her children admission, and she filed a lawsuit in
the Kansas Supreme Court against the Board of Education. According to Wright,
an agreement was made between Rich and the Topeka board that provided that if
she "disclaimed any discrimination or prejudice against her children ... that the
Board of Education would in such event immediately remove from attendance at

Randolph School the children of George Wright" (*Wright*, Counter Abstract and Brief of Appellees 1930, 4). The Board of Education denied making such an agreement. Soon afterward, the Board of Education started providing and "maintaining a bus service without charge to pupils or to parents of pupils, by which a bus traveling on a certain route is provided to take these colored children from various parts of the city and deliver them to Buchanan School" (*Wright*, Counter Abstract and Brief of Appellees 1930, 5).

The Topeka Board of Education issued the following order on January 7, 1929: "The colored children still attending Randolph and Gage Park Schools be permitted to continue attending those schools until the end of the semester, January 25th, 1929 and thereafter be transferred to Buchanan" (*Wright*, Abstract of Record 1930, 10). The reason for this order was that:

> Randolph School is and always has been maintained exclusively for white children, while Buchanan is and always has been maintained by the defendant Board exclusively for colored children and said defendants acting in the utmost good faith and for what they deemed to be the best interest of both the colored and white children have attempted to separate said races in the lower grades. (*Wright*, Counter Abstract and Brief of Appellees 1930, 10–11)

On January 22, 1929, G. L. Coleman, the principal of Randolph School, and A. J. Stout, the superintendent of public schools of Topeka, informed William Wright that at the end of the current term his children would be transferred to Buchanan School. In order to reach Buchanan school, Wilhemina would have to travel two miles. The district court issued a restraining order on February 2, 1929, restraining the school board, principal, and superintendent from transferring Wilhemina Wright and Preston Trice from Randolph School to Buchanan School.[4]

Eugene S. Quinton represented the Wrights and presented two arguments to the court. The first argument was based on the contractual arrangement Wright had with the Board of Education at the time the College Hill area was annexed into the city of Topeka. This oral agreement provided that Wrights's children, including those not yet in school, would be permitted to continue to attend school in District 22 until they graduated.

The second argument made by Quinton pertained to the distance that Wilhemina would have to travel in order to reach Buchanan. Quinton argued that Wilhemina would have to cross twenty streets in order to arrive at Buchanan School, and these streets were "constantly filled with the most potent hazards, the automobile traffic, especially at morning, noon and night" (*Wright*, Abstract of Record 1930, 3). Because the practice at that time was for children to return home at noon for lunch, Quinton contended that each day Wilhemina would have to walk eight miles and cross 106 public streets. He also proposed that, given the two mile distance, it would be impracticable for her to return home for lunch.

With regard to the bus transportation the Board of Education provided to the children, Quinton argued that the children's health was threatened because the bus did not follow a regular schedule, and no shelter was provided to shield the children from inclement weather. Both facts, the walking distance and the inadequacy of the bus service, constituted an unnecessary hardship and subjected "them to perils so obvious and great that their parents would not permit them to incur the hazard necessarily and unavoidably involved in attending [Buchanan] School" (*Wright*, Counter Abstract and Brief of Appellees 1930, 20). In making this argument, Quinton relied on the Supreme Court's first opinion in *Williams v. Board of Education of the City of Parsons* (1908).

The city of Topeka Board of Education was represented by five attorneys: Bennett R. Wheeler, S. M. Brewster, John L. Hunt, Virgil V. Scholes, and Margaret McGurnaghan. The Board of Education members denied that they had entered into an agreement with Mr. Wright that would have allowed his children to continue to attend school in District No. 22. They contended that they had not authorized Mr. Duggins to act on their behalf and that he lacked the authority to bind them to an agreement with Wright. They also argued that even if such an agreement had been made, it "was illegal and void and not binding upon the defendants" (*Wright*, Counter Abstract and Brief of Appellees 1930, 8). Although they admitted that Mr. Wright's children had been allowed to attend Randolph School for the past two years, their attendance was not due to any agreement between the parties.

With regard to the contract between the Board of Education and Maude Rich, the Board of Education denied that an agreement was reached in that case that would have allowed Wright's children to continue to attend Randolph School. They did admit they "entered into a stipulation whereby certain portions of the application for writ of mandamus were eliminated" (*Wright*, Counter Abstract and Brief of Appellees 1930, 8). However, they did not reveal the terms of this stipulation.

The attorneys for the Board of Education addressed the issue of the distance from the Wrights's home to Buchanan School by pointing out that it provided bus transportation to Wilhemina and that the "bus service furnishe[d] good, clean, commodious, safe and prompt transportation" (*Wright*, Counter Abstract and Brief of Appellees 1930, 9). They denied the bus transportation subjected her "to any peril, hazards, impending dangers, risks of severe and probable injuries, or undue exposure to the weather" (*Wright*, Counter Abstract and Brief of Appellees 1930, 9–10). In support of their position regarding the safety of the bus transportation, the Board of Education pointed out that there had been no accidents since the Topeka Railway Company started providing bus transportation in February 1925.

The Board of Education denied that by sending Wilhemina Wright to Buchanan she was "deprived of [her right] of the equal protection and enjoyment of educational facilities guaranteed ... under the Constitution of the State of Kansas" (*Wright*, Counter Abstract and Brief of Appellees 1930, 10). Buchanan School was "a comparatively new building, in excellent condition, and is modern in every respect, and has the same type of heating and ventilation systems as used in Randolph" (*Wright*, Counter Abstract and Brief of Appellees 1930, 11). They noted that Buchanan was superior to some of the schools in the city established exclusively for White children.

Drawing from forty-plus years of experience, the Board of Education articulated the following reasons why maintaining separate schools for White and Black children was in the best interest of both.

1. Prevents friction between children of such age and is conducive to better scholastic attainment and better spirit on the part of both colored and white children;
2. Separation of colored children into separate schools permits such children to have the benefit of colored teachers, who are especially adapted to teach colored children and who are conversant with, appreciate and understand their problems and difficulties better than white teachers;
3. Separation tends to develop leadership among the colored children;
4. Colored teachers of Buchanan School are excellent teachers, each being certified by the State of Kansas to teach in public schools. (*Wright*, Counter Abstract and Brief of Appellees 1930, 11)

It is interesting to note that once again the Topeka Board of Education identified preventing friction and quarrels as a rationale for establishing separate schools; however, they once again failed to present evidence of friction or quarrels between the White and Black children when they attended the same school.

In the brief he filed with the Supreme Court, Quinton characterized the order of the district court as "an inhuman enforcement of the law ... for no offense or reason on earth except that she is a colored girl" (Brief of Appellant, *Wright v. Board of Education of Topeka* 1930 [hereinafter Wright, *Brief of Appellant*], 1, 2). Quinton did not raise the issue of the contractual agreement in his appeal to the Supreme Court. The only issue he presented for consideration was whether "the defendant's order that the plaintiff attend school at Buchanan school [was] unreasonable, in view of the distance she have to go and the street intersections she would be compelled to cross" (*Wright v. Board of Education of Topeka* 1930, 363). Quinton conceded that first-class cities were authorized to operate separate schools for Black and White children; however, he urged the court to apply the rule of law pronounced in *Williams v. Board of Education of City of Parsons.*

> Where children entitled to school privileges in a city, if required to attend a certain school designated by the board of education, would be exposed to daily dangers to life and limb so obvious and so great that in the exercise of reasonable prudence their parents should not permit them to incur the hazard necessarily and unavoidably involved in such attendance, they should not be compelled to attend the school so designated. (*Wright*, Brief of Appellant 1930, 2)

Quinton argued the that distance and path that Wilhemina must walk to Buchanan School was so dangerous that it denied her access to "equal educational facilities" and that the Board of Education's assignment of Wilhemina to Buchanan was an "abuse of discretion" (*Wright*, Brief of Appellant 1930, 3). Quinton did not address the fact that the Board of Education had provided bus transportation to Buchanan for the children residing in that area of Topeka. Quinton argued that, given the danger, enforcement of the district court's order would be inhumane.

The Board of Education argued their assignment of Wilhemina Wright to Buchanan School did not infringe on her rights because the board had ensured her safety by providing transportation to the school at no expense to her parents. The board also pointed out that "there [was] no suggestion that the colored school provided for [Wilhemina Wright] was not equal in every way to the white school which she desired to attend" (*Wright*, Counter Abstract and Brief of Defendant 1930, 29). Therefore, the only issue was an objection to the board assigning her to attend Buchanan.

The board attacked Quinton's reliance on the *Williams* case based on the fact that when the Kansas Supreme Court considered the case on it merits, it had ruled:

> The control of city schools, including selection of sites and the distribution of pupils is devolved upon the board of education. The discretion committed to that body is to be exercised, as was said in the opinion denying the motion to quash 'untrammeled by judicial interference.' (*Wright*, Counter Abstract and Brief of Defendant 1930, 30)

The action of the board was clearly within its authority, and it was reasonable that the exercise of its power to assign pupils would result in both White and Black pupils having to travel farther than some of their peers.

The Kansas Supreme Court issued a one-page opinion written by Justice Harvey. In examining the issue raised by the plaintiff that requiring Wilhemina Wright to walk two miles to school presented a dangerous condition such that the actions of the Board of Education was unreasonable, the Kansas Supreme Court upheld the district court's decision and stated:

> This contention is taken out of the case when we examine the pleadings for the plaintiff, for the plaintiff alleged that defendant furnishes transportation by automobile bus for plaintiff to and from the Buchanan school without expense to her or her parents, and the answer of defendant admitted that it does so. There is no contention that this transportation is not adequate, appropriate or sufficient. (*Wright v. Board of Education of Topeka* 1930, 363)

The Supreme Court determined that providing transportation to Buchanan School alleviated any dangerous condition that might have existed were Wilhemina required to walk to school and that the board had properly exercised the powers granted to it by the state legislature.

Graham v. Board of Education of Topeka **(1941)**

On January 29, 1940, Oaland Graham, Jr., presented himself for admission to Boswell Junior High School in the first-class city of Topeka. The previous school term, he had attended grade 6A at Buchanan School and on January 26, 1940, was promoted to grade 7B. Charles S. Todd, the Boswell principal, denied him admission to Boswell Junior High School on the basis of his race. The same day Oaland was denied admission to Boswell Junior High School, Ulysses A. Graham filed a writ of mandamus in the Kansas Supreme Court seeking the admission of his son Oaland to Boswell Junior High School.

The city of Topeka Board of Education operated a dual junior high school system, which resulted in White-only seventh and eighth grades. The educational model adopted for the White children was a *six-three-three plan*, which was used to classify and to assign the White students to the appropriate grade. The application of this plan resulted in White students attending elementary school for the first six grades, then attending a junior high school for the next three grades, and spending the last three grades in a high school. With regard to the Black children, the Board of Education adopted what Graham referred to as an *eight-one-three* plan. Pursuant to this plan, the Black children attended an elementary school for the first eight grades, then attended the White junior high school for the ninth grade and, like the White children, went to the high school for their last three grades.

William A. Bradshaw represented the Grahams. Bradshaw raised the following questions for the court's consideration:

(1) Is Boswell Junior High School in the City of Topeka, Kansas, as organized, a high school within the meaning of [the law authorizing first-class cities to segregate education and the law authorizing the establishment of junior high schools]?

(2) Can the defendants deny the plaintiff enrollment and school instruction in the 7B grade in Boswell Junior High School in the City of Topeka, Kansas, when the evidence discloses that the educational advantages offered in the 7B grade in the Buchanan School, an elementary school for colored students only, are not equivalent to the educational advantages offered in the same grade in Boswell Junior High School? (Brief of Plaintiff, *Graham v. Board of Education of Topeka* 1941 [hereinafter Graham, *Brief of Plaintiff*], 1–2)

The first question sought an expansion of the definition of *junior high school*, which had been provided in the *Thurman-Watts* decision (*Thurman-Watts v. Board of Education*, 1924). The second question provided an alternate route on which the court could make a decision that would permit Oaland Graham, Jr., access to Boswell Junior High School. Although the second question addressed issues of equal educational opportunities, the impact of a Kansas Supreme Court decision on this question would have only a local impact (i.e., the educational facilities provided to Black junior high school students in Topeka were not equal to those provided to the White students of Topeka). However, if the Kansas Supreme Court expanded the definition of *high school* to include junior high schools, then the decision would have a statewide impact and would have narrowed the scope of segregated education in Kansas. By adding seventh and eighth grades to the definition of *high school*, first-class cities would have authority to segregate Black and White children only through the sixth grade, rather than through the eighth grade.

In making the argument that junior high schools were high schools, Bradshaw argued the "organization, administration, and method of instruction, the junior high school [was] identical in all respects to the senior high school" (*Graham*, Brief of Plaintiff 1941, 11). In support of this argument, Bradshaw relied on the rules adopted by the State Board of Education as published in the *Biennial Report of the Superintendent of Public Instruction*, as well as the *Handbook on Organization and Practices for Secondary Schools of Kansas*. One section of the Biennial Report, entitled "Growth of the Kansas High Schools" stated that "the secondary school program has been reorganized to include the junior high school" (State Superintendent of Public Instruction 1938, 18). The *Handbook on Organization and Practices for Secondary Schools of Kansas* required junior high schools to submit reports in the same manner as high schools and, where applicable, the high school standards for accreditation were used for junior high schools.

The second issue presented by Bradshaw pertained to whether the eight-one-three plan afforded Black children the same educational advantages as the six-three-three plan available only to the White children. He argued "there [were] at least seventeen substantial educational advantages ... offered to White students in Boswell Junior High School in the 7B grade during 1940 that were not offered to colored students in Buchanan" (Graham, Brief of Plaintiff 1941, 22). Bradshaw offered the following reasons as indicative of the superior education provided through the use of the six-three-three plan: departmentalized curriculum, more advanced grading system, extracurricular activities (instrumental music, athletics, and swimming), and facilities (gymnasium and auditorium).

In support of his legal argument, Bradshaw cited the *Williams* case. He also relied on the U.S. Supreme Court decision in *State of Missouri ex. rel. Gaines v. Canada*, which was the first education-related legal battled waged by the NAACP in the federal courts. In this case, Lloyd Gaines sought admission to the University of Missouri law school. He was denied admission, not because he was unqualified but because of a state statute prohibiting integrated education. He brought suit alleging that Missouri had failed to provide him with separate but equal educational opportunities. Missouri argued that the provisions of the state law, which would pay tuition for Gaines to attend law school out of state, passed the requirements of *Plessy*. The Supreme Court ruled in favor of Gaines, stating that Gaines had not been provided with equal protection of the laws. The court held that although it was permissible for Missouri to require Blacks to attend separate law schools, in order for the legal education to be equal it must be received within the state in which the individual wished to practice law. Bradshaw also cited *Pearson v. Murray*, another U.S. Supreme Court decision. The court held that Maryland violated the 14th Amendment by failing to admit Murray to the University of Maryland law school.

Bradshaw relied on the following precedent:

> where the schools for each race do not furnish similar courses of study or where the provisions for such similar courses do not permit them to be followed under circumstances of equal advantage, it has been generally held that there are not equivalent educational facilities. (*Pearson v. Murray* 1938, 717)

The differences between the educational advantages offered the White students at Boswell and those afforded the Black children at Buchanan were so vastly different that the Topeka Board of Education failed to provide "equal advantage" and "equivalent educational facilities" to the Black children assigned to the 7B grade. Bradshaw argued that the differences between the educational facilities at Boswell and Buchanan also resulted in unjust discrimination against the Black children.

The Topeka Board of Education was represented by J. L. Hunt, Lester M. Goodell, Margaret McGurnaghan, John H. Hunt, and George M. Brewster. Topeka provided the following reasons supporting its argument that the seventh and eighth grades were elementary grades and not high school grades. The first reason was that the court must interpret the term by using the meaning of the word at the time the statute was adopted. The statute in question was adopted in 1905. According to the board, California established the first junior high school in 1910. It was 1913 or 1914 before Kansas established junior high schools and "the first junior high school in Topeka was organized in 1914 or 1915" (Brief of Defendant, *Graham v. Board of Education of Topeka* 1941 [hereinafter Graham, *Brief of Defendant*], 60). Therefore, at the time the Kansas legislature adopted the statute it could not have intended to include the seventh and eighth grades in its meaning of high school. The defendants relied on the *Thurman-Watts* decision, in which the Kansas Supreme Court "clearly held that the words 'high school' as used in the statute under consideration meant the four years of study immediately following the first eight grades, regardless of whether the 6-3-3 or junior high school plan was in use or not" (*Graham*, Brief of Defendant 1941, 61). Therefore, junior high schools were not high schools, and Topeka was authorized to segregate the seventh and eighth grades.

The Topeka Board of Education argued "the court must bear in mind that *difference alone does not mean discrimination*. There must not only be a difference but there must be a showing of inequality and advantage of one over the other before there can be discrimination" (*Graham*, Brief of Defendant 1941, 63). The Topeka board reminded the court that it had stated in *Reynolds* that "equality and not identity of privileges and rights is what is guaranteed to citizens" (*Reynolds v. Board of Education of Topeka* 1903, 692). The board proposed Graham had failed to prove that substantial inequalities existed and further argued that none existed. The board took the position that the children at Buchanan received educational opportunities that were equal to those provided to the children at Boswell and that any differences that existed with regard to curricula and facilities were not substantial enough to warrant a finding by the court of inequality.

The Kansas Supreme Court announced its decision on June 13, 1941. The Kansas Supreme Court considered the issue of the provision of equal educational facilities first and found that Topeka's dual system of junior high schools discriminated against the Black children and failed to provide them with equal educational advantages. Justice Allen wrote:

> The school authorities of the city are not required to furnish the benefits of a departmentalized junior high school to its residents, but they cannot be furnished to white children residing within a particular district and be withheld from negro children residing in the same district and having equal qualifications because of their race. (*Graham v. Board of Education of Topeka* 1941)

The court found that the departmentalized plan, as well as the differences in facilities and extracurricular activities, afforded the White children an advantage over the Black children. The court stated "the junior high school method of departmentalization is considered to be an advanced and improved method of education" (*Graham v. Board of Education of Topeka* 1941, 317) and distinguished the *Reynolds* case because the facts in *Reynolds* did not reveal any differences with regard to curricula or method of instruction. The *Reynolds* case dealt solely with the issue of the newness and size of the new school provided for the White children.

The Kansas Supreme Court did disagree with Graham's argument that junior high schools should be considered high schools and as such could not be segregated. Because the junior high schools did not exist at the time the statute was enacted, the legislature could not have intended to include junior high schools within the definition of *high schools*. The Kansas Supreme Court stated that "It would seem to be established that the legislature by the use of the word high school in this statute meant to include the grades commonly recognized as high school grades namely, the ninth, tenth, eleventh, and twelfth grades" (*Reynolds v. Board of Education of Topeka* 1903, 318). The court relied on its previous decision in *Thurman-Watts* to support this definition of *high school*.

Unlike the previous decisions of the court, which had been unanimous, Justice Harvey issued a separate opinion. Although he concurred with the court in its determination that Topeka had failed to provide the Black students with equal educational facilities and opportunities, he disagreed with the court's interpretation of the meaning of *high school*. Harvey proposed that the court should apply the meaning of that term as it existed in 1868, rather than 1905, because this was the year of the original enactment of the statute authorizing first-class cities to establish separate schools for White and Black children. Harvey argued the statute had always provided school boards with the power to specify how students were to be classified and to determine which grades should be included in high schools. He pointed out that common schools in the 1870s and 1880s "usually consisted of five grades … so, to start a high school at even as early as the sixth grade was neither unheard of nor unlawful" (*Graham v. Board of Education of Topeka* 1941, 319). Harvey believed that the junior high school system as used in Topeka resulted in a reorganization of Topeka's high school system. He claimed that the Topeka Board of Education "voluntarily took advantage of [the statute that allowed the organization of junior high schools] and remodeled its school structure so as to provide such high schools for all the white children of the city, but not for the colored children" (*Graham v. Board of Education of Topeka* 1941, 320). Because he believed junior high schools were high schools, Harvey dissented from the court's decision holding that first-class cities were authorized to segregate junior high schools because they were not part of the high school system.

Lessons Learned From Topeka

The fiftieth anniversary of the U.S. Supreme Court decision in *Brown v. Board of Education of Topeka, Kansas*, gave cause for a time to reflect on the progress that has been made with regard to equal educational opportunities for disenfranchised groups in the United States. For many, these reflections led to the conclusion that the goal of equal education still has not been obtained. As alluded to in the beginning of this article, the lawyers involved in the *Brown* case identified its role with regard to the issue of the constitutionality of separate education as a factor that made it unique from the other four cases, which collectively made up the *Brown* decision. Although legally sanctioned segregation was a serious problem that needed to be addressed, in the context of educational practices the treatment of segregation as the primary legal issue, rather than inequitable educational practices, influenced the crafting of legal remedies. According to Virgil A. Clift, "the issue of segregation was to be regarded as an important part of the problem, but it was not to be regarded as the whole of the problem, nor even as the central issue. Even if, by some miracle, every school in the country could be desegregated overnight, the basic problem … would still remain. This basic problem is that of providing equality of educational opportunity" (Clift, Archibald, and Hullfish 1962, xi).

Reynolds, Wright and *Graham* provided insights into how the Kansas legal system responded to the issue of segregated education. Although the courts recognized the authority of first-class cities to establish separate schools for Black and White children, it also placed importance on ensuring that the educational opportunities provided were equal. However, the Kansas Supreme Court decisions were limited in their scope. For example, in *Reynolds*, the court determined that the mandate of equality was satisfied by the provision of substantially equal school advantages and stated that equality of rights was not synonymous with identical rights. In *Graham* that court found only that the junior high school system as it was in place in Topeka failed to provide Oaland Graham, Jr., with equal educational advantages. The court sidestepped making its decision applicable to all junior high schools in Kansas by refusing to adopt a definition of *junior high school* that would have made it part of the high school structure of schooling in Kansas, thereby limiting the applicability of this decision to Topeka alone.

However, these decisions did lay the groundwork for the legal issues addressed in *Brown* in that they assisted in the establishment of a context that was amenable to legal challenges to segregated education and provided equal educational advantages to its Black school-age children. The NAACP found in Topeka a Black community that was willing to confront segregated education. The NAACP had first targeted a case out of Johnson County, *Webb v. School District No. 90, Johnson County, State of Kansas* (1949), as part of its campaign to challenge segregated education in elementary and secondary schools. However, the Kansas Supreme Court's decision left no grounds for appeal. The court held that Johnson County School District No. 90 had, for generations, operated segregated schools without legislative authority to do so and concluded that the school district's action of gerrymandering the lines for the attendance zones was a clear act of subterfuge. It ordered the school district to admit all of the school-age children to South Park District School for the 1949–1950 school year. Because the Kansas Supreme Court decided this case solely on the grounds of state law and did not address the federal constitutional issues, an appeal to the U.S. Supreme Court was foreclosed. If *Webb* had been decided in favor of the school district, it is likely that it would have appeared on the Supreme Court's docket instead of the *Brown* case out of Topeka. The NAACP then focused its efforts on Wichita, Kansas; however, it encountered resistance from Black teachers and was unable to garner enough support for a legal challenge. Turning to Topeka, the NAACP found not only a local community ready to challenge segregated education but also a legal history that resulted in the mandate that separate education in Topeka provide equal educational advantages. Without Topeka and without *Brown,* the Supreme Court's decision on May 17, 1954, may have had a different result.

Notes

1. This document is archived in the Spencer Library, University of Kansas.
2. It should be noted that *Board of Education of Ottawa v. Tinnon*, 26 Kan 1 (1881),was the first state legal decision to challenge segregated education in Kansas. However, in this paper I focus solely on the three legal decisions prior to *Brown* involving Topeka, Kansas.
3. There were only four states that had laws that permitted education in varying degrees: Kansas, Wyoming, New Mexico and Arizona.
4. By the time this case reached the Supreme Court, Wright's son, Preston Trice, completed the sixth grade and was promoted to the seventh grade housed in another school.

References

Abstract of Record, *Wright v. Board of Education of Topeka*. 1930. Kansas State Supreme Court Records, Case No. 29, 324. Topeka: Kansas State Historical Society.

Board of Education of Ottawa v. Tinnon, 26 Kan 1 (1881).

Brief of Appellant, *Wright v. Board of Education of Topeka*. 1930. Kansas State Supreme Court Records, Case No. 29, 324. Topeka: Kansas State Historical Society.

Brief of Defendant, *Graham v. Board of Education of Topeka*. 1903. Kansas State Supreme Court Records, Case No. 34, 791. Topeka: Kansas State Historical Society.

Brief of Defendant, *Reynolds v. Board of Education of Topeka*. 1903. Kansas State Supreme Court Records, Case No. 13, 140. Topeka: Kansas State Historical Society.

Brief of Plaintiff, *Graham v. Board of Education of Topeka*. 1941. Kansas State Supreme Court Records, Case No. 34, 791. Topeka: Kansas State Historical Society.

Brief of Plaintiff, *Reynolds v. Board of Education of Topeka*. 1903. Kansas State Supreme Court Records, Case No. 13, 140. Topeka: Kansas State Historical Society.

Brown v. Board of Education of Topeka, Kansas, 98 F. Supp. 797, 347 U. S. 483 (1954).

Clift, Virgil A., Archibald W. Anderson, and H. Gordon Hullfish, eds. 1962. *Negro Education in America: Its Adequacy, Problems and Needs*. New York: Harper and Brothers Publishers.

Counter Abstract and Brief of Appellees, *Wright v. Board of Education of Topeka*. 1930. Kansas State Supreme Court Records, Case No. 29, 324. Topeka: Kansas State Historical Society.

Cox, Thomas C. 1982. *Blacks in Topeka, Kansas: 1865–1915*. Baton Rouge: Louisiana State University Press.

Graham v. Board of Education of Topeka, 114 P2d 313 (Kan. 1941).

Graham v. Board of Education of Topeka. 1941. Kansas State Supreme Court Records, Case No. 34, 791. Topeka: Kansas State Historical Society.

Missouri, ex. rel. Gaines v. Canada, 305 U.S. 337 (1938).

Painter, Nell Irvin. [1976] 1986. *Exodusters: Black Migration to Kansas After Reconstruction*. New York: W.W. Norton and Company.

Pearson v. Murray, 103 A.L.R. 706, 717 (1938).

Plessy v. Ferguson, 163 US 537 (1896).

Reynolds v. Board of Education of Topeka, 72 P 274 (Kan. 1903).

Reynolds v. Board of Education of Topeka. 1903. Kansas State Supreme Court Records, Case No. 13, 140. Topeka: Kansas State Historical Society.

State Superintendent of Public Instruction. 1938. *Thirty-First Biennial Report*. Topeka, Kansas: State Printing Office.

Supplemental Brief for Defendant, *Reynolds v. Board of Education of Topeka*. 1903. Kansas State Supreme Court Records, Box No. 13, 140. Topeka: Kansas State Historical Society.

Thurman–Watts v. Board of Education, 222 P 123, 125 (Kan. 1924).

Webb v. School District No. 90, Johnson County et al., 206 P2d 1066 (Kan. 1949).

Williams v. Board of Education of City of Parsons, 99 P 216, 217 (Kan. 1908).

Williams v. Board of Education of Parsons, 106 P 36 (1910).

Wilson, Paul E. 1995. *A Time to Lose: Representing Kansas in* Brown v. Board of Education. Lawrence: University of Kansas Press.

Wright v. Board of Education of Topeka, 284 P 363 (Kan. 1930).

Wright v. Board of Education of Topeka. 1930. Kansas State Supreme Court Records, Case No. 29, 324. Topeka: Kansas State Historical Society.

Correspondence should be addressed to Jamie B. Lewis, College of Education, 122 Aderhold Hall, Athens, GA 30602. E-mail: jlewis@coe.uga.edu

INTERVIEW

In Their Words: A Living History of the Brown Decision

JUDITH LYNNE McCONNELL
Washburn University

BLYTHE F. HINITZ
The College of New Jersey

"I feel like a winner" was the recollection of Mrs. Vivian Scales as she reflected on hearing the Supreme Court's decision in the *Brown v. Board of Education of Topeka, Kansas*, case on May 17, 1954. Scales was one of the original plaintiffs who challenged the existence of separate elementary schools for African American and White students in Topeka. Excerpts of interviews conducted with Mrs. Scales and Rev. Oliver Browns' daughters, Linda Brown Thompson and Cheryl Brown Henderson, are referenced in commemoration of the 50th anniversary of the *Brown* decision.

A Brief History of Segregation and Attempts to Integrate in Topeka, Kansas

Topeka of the early 1950s was quite different from Topeka, Kansas, today. In the early 1950s, Topeka was a city of seventy-nine thousand citizens, with an African American population of 7 percent, or a little more than five thousand people. The African American population lived in four sections of Topeka: Mudtown, an area earlier known as Redmonsville, The Bottoms, and Tennessee Town. This last area of Topeka, Tennessee Town, was settled in the late 1870s by approximately three thousand *exodusters*, as the former slaves were called (McConnell 1995). The exodusters had left the Mississippi Valley, often sponsored by White church congregations, with promises of cheap land and their safety in the western states.

The Central Congregational Church in Topeka was instrumental in improving the living conditions of the African Americans living in Tennessee Town. One of the social reforms conducted by its pastor, Dr. Charles Sheldon, was the founding of a kindergarten in 1893. This was the first kindergarten west of the Mississippi River for African American children. The most prominent alumnus of the Tennessee Town kindergarten was Elisha Scott, in whom Sheldon took a special interest and for whom he arranged, years later, support to attend law school at Washburn University. Scott became a leading Topeka attorney, as did his sons, John Scott and Charles Sheldon Scott. The Scotts argued many civil rights and school desegregation cases. Their most illustrious moment came in 1954 when Charles Sheldon Scott argued the winning side of the landmark *Brown v. Board of Education of Topeka, Kansas*, desegregation case before the U.S. Supreme Court (Miller 1986).

In the early 1950s, the high school in Topeka was integrated, although there were eighteen elementary schools strictly designed for Whites and four elementary schools designated for African Americans. The African American elementary schools were Monroe, Washington, McKinley, and Buchanan. In these schools students were taught from the age of kindergarten through eighth grade. White students could attend their neighborhood elementary schools, yet their African American neighbors had to ride a school bus to an African American elementary school. Some African American students walked to school, as seen in the often-published photograph of Linda Brown walking across the railroad tracks on her way to the bus stop from which she rode a school bus to school. Although some students did walk to school, most African American students, like Linda, walked to bus stops where buses would transport them to their segregated elementary schools. Several parents of African American students were disturbed by this practice, including Mrs. Vivian Scales. Her fourth-grade daughter, Ruth, was bused to an African American school far from her neighborhood. Mrs. Scales, Rev. Oliver Brown, and eleven other parents took decisive action so their children could attend their neighborhood elementary schools, and consequently they were the plaintiffs from Kansas in the *Brown* case.

Interview With Mrs. Vivian Scales

A more personal version of the landmark *Brown* decision comes from original sources. In November 1998, a rare opportunity arose when Mrs. Vivian Scales, one of the few remaining plaintiffs in the *Brown* case, granted an interview in her east Topeka home. The following passages come from the record of this interview.

Interviewer: What triggered your involvement in what became the *Brown v. Topeka Board of Education* decision? How did it all begin?

Scales: Mr. Burnett was President of NAACP [National Association for the Advancement of Colored People] and encouraged a group of us women in this *Brown* thing. He talked about how we could expect to be treated and what might happen. He mentioned it at a parent–teacher meeting and he was very anxious [that we should become involved].

Interviewer: What about the initial meetings of the parents who were going to be involved as plaintiffs in this case?

Scales: The men [fathers] had two jobs and kept the kids while we went to the meetings. We was churchgoers and we knew how to stay out of trouble. Just mothers were at the meetings. We met at the post office in the Justice Room. I went there rain, sleet or shine. The African American teachers were disturbed about losing their jobs, because the principal at Washington Elementary School told them that if they participated they would lose their jobs. A lot [of them] did what he asked.

Interviewer: What did you tell your daughter about attempting to register her in the school?

Scales: The children were prepared. The paper said the schools were to enroll today. They [NAACP] said to take someone with you that wasn't part of the decision. I went to Parkdale to register Ruth and I thought she'd [the secretary] run. The principal refused us.

Interviewer: What are some of the little-known facts, things that happened during that time?

Scales: They [NAACP] were confident that they would win.

Interviewer: What was the atmosphere like here in Topeka during the Supreme Court trial?

Scales: A little stressful. We were churchgoing people and didn't put up with anything wrong. It [segregation] was wrong.

Interviewer: What was it like in Topeka when the verdict was announced?

Scales: It was so exciting—everybody was outside in the neighborhood. We'd come a long, long way! Not much stress after the case, some people just won't change. The next day we went to the dollar store and sat at the counter and order a soda. It impacted everything, 'cause restaurants served us only from the back door in paper sacks [before the decision].

Interviewer: Were there any repercussions to the African American community in Topeka?

Scales: Never had any incidents. Never had any, it depends on how you carry yourself.

Interviewer: How did you feel about Reverence [*sic*] Brown being listed as the major party in the case?

Scales: Can't figure how and why to this day. They called it Linda Brown. Never did understand that, I guess it's because Oliver Brown was the only man.

Interviewer: How was schooling different for your children after the decision?

Scales: Black people have always had it different. Very few Whites went to the Black schools after the decision. The White parents, they had cars and took their kids to other schools.

Interviewer: How do you feel the decision has impacted Topeka now[,] more than forty years later?

Scales: A big difference. All of the Black schools are closed. The jobs changed. The service changed. Will never be equal because there are some White people that won't go with the Black kids. It is a big day that they closed all of the Black schools.

Interviewer: Was it worth it? Would you help initiate the case all over again?

Scales: Every bit of it. Yes, my daughter had a better life because of it. I feel like a winner. I'm for whatever is right.

Interview With the Brown Sisters: As They Remember

The Reverend Oliver Brown died in 1961. In September of 1998, his daughters, Cheryl Brown Henderson and her sister, Linda Brown Thompson, shared their views on situations leading up to and during the *Brown* case. Both sisters responded to prepared written questions; in addition, they graciously allowed students in an undergraduate course at Washburn University to ask them questions, as seen in the following excerpts.

Interviewer: From a child's standpoint, how did you feel being singled out for such a test case?

Thompson: Because I was a minor (eight years old) I played a very limited role in what happened at the time. I did appear in court but did not have to testify. My father, of course, provided the testimony about my circumstances [i.e., having to attend Monroe Elementary School instead of the neighborhood elementary school four blocks away].

Henderson: The most I remember is that when the parents involved tried to enroll us in the all-White school and we were denied, my mother explained that it was because of the color of our skin. As a child I did not comprehend what difference that could possibly make.

Interviewer: Why did your parents think the school you attended wasn't equal to others in Topeka? Can you give specific examples?

Thompson: The Topeka case was not about inequality. It was about equal access. The schools for Black children were built by the same companies as those for White children. The teaching staff and materials were also equal with regard to their education and of subjects taught. In fact, one of the all-Black schools, Washington Elementary School, had more teachers with master's degrees than any school in the city.

Henderson: The issue for Black parents was the distance their children had to travel to attend school, when there were schools in their neighborhood. Neighborhoods in Topeka were integrated. People lived where they could afford to live.

Interviewer: What improvements in education today do you feel are a result of your parents' willingness to stand up for your rights?

Thompson: We believe for our parents and others it took courage to get involved and to agree to participate. They ran the risk of loosing jobs or personal injury. They believed what they were doing was right. This was a case put together by the NAACP and attorneys who then asked parents with elementary-age children to participate.

Henderson: We believe the results have been seen more in other areas of society, such as, public accommodations, which were some of the most segregated situations. Education has been slow to comply. The greatest improvement is an understanding of all people by learning about cultures different than our own. Multicultural education was unheard of before this took place.

The Legacy Begun in Topeka 50 years Ago Continues...

It is true the impact of the *Brown* decision remains a link between past, present, and future generations of Americans who strive for equality. In 1957, Dr. Martin Luther King, Jr., held a prayer pilgrimage to mark the third anniversary of the decision, and in that same year there was an attempt to integrate Central High School in Little Rock, Arkansas. In 1958, lunch counter sit-ins began in several major cities, and during the early 1960s other nonviolent actions were staged through out the

United States. The culmination of all of these efforts was the passage of the historic Civil Rights legislation of 1964. As educators, we know that which impacts on the field of education often has a far-reaching effect to other segments of society. Reverend Oliver Brown, Mrs. Vivian Scales, and the other 11 parents demonstrated by their courageous actions that ordinary American citizens can significantly alter the lives of their children and future generations.

References

McConnell, Judith L. 1995. "Kindergarten in Kansas: A View from the Beginning." *Journal of Education* 177:9–22.

Miller, Timothy. 1986. Charles M. Sheldon and the Uplift of Tennessee Town. *Kansas History: A Journal of the Central Plains* 9:125–137.

Correspondence should be addressed to Judith McConnell, Washburn University, 1700 SW College Ave., Topeka, KS 66621. E-mail: judy.mcconnell@washburn.edu

BOOK REVIEWS

Sons of Mississippi: A Story of Race Relations and Its Legacy. Paul Hendrickson. New York: Alfred A Knopf, 2003. 368 pp. $26.00 (cloth), $15.00 (paper).

NANCY LASHER and JAYNE ZANGLEIN
The College of New Jersey

"People really don't change in their prejudice, not underneath, in their true character. It's the rarest exception, when someone really converts." Mississippi Judge Mary Toles, quoted in *Sons of Mississippi* (Hendrickson, 254).

"A very covert system [is] in place now. You see, [racism] is more vicious now because it's largely unseen." Joseph Meredith, son of James Meredith, 2002, quoted in *Sons of Mississippi* (Hendrickson, 304–305).

The fiftieth anniversary of *Brown v. Board of Education of Topeka, Kansas,* provides an opportunity for educators and policymakers to examine educational reform through a critical lens. Paul Hendrickson's *Sons of Mississippi*, which was written on the eve of another anniversary—the fortieth anniversary of the integration of Ole Miss by James Meredith—offers the reader the singular opportunity to examine racial hatred, tolerance, and moral ambivalence through the eyes of photographer Charles Moore, the seven lawmen he photographed, and their children. It is a story of orchestrated deception and duplicity.

Sons of Mississippi chronicles the lives of seven Mississippi sheriffs who rallied together on the campus of the University of Mississippi to control the mobs of angry Mississippians who were expected to protest against the admission of James Meredith. The sheriffs flocked to the campus to defend their way of life. Self-appointed defenders of the law of nature and the law of God, the sheriffs were intent on preserving "racial purity" and maintaining "Anglo-Saxon institutions" such as White supremacy (308). As Hendrickson describes the sheriffs, "[T] hey're on a mission from God. They're confronting history, and they know it" (18).

What the sheriffs don't know is that they have already lost not only the battle but also the war against integration. They don't realize that they are, in a sense, the "ex-

Mississippi, 1962 (*Source*: Photograph by Charles Moore, available at http://www.kodak.com/US/en/corp/features/moore/lawmenFrame.shtml)

tras" on the theatrical set. The politicians have scripted the scene and know that segregation is about to fall. They know this is the sheriffs' last stand against integration. But the sheriffs are oblivious to the end of an era and regard Ole Miss as the first battle in a war that will be waged across the state.

While the politicians are inside negotiating when and how to concede, the sheriffs are outside getting ready to incite the crowds. As the men prepare for battle, they gather around Sheriff Billy Ferrell, president of the Mississippi Sheriffs' Association, who is practicing his batting strokes. That moment—of Ferrell swinging the billy club, cigarette clenched in his mouth, grinning, and surrounded by his fellow lawmen who are rooting him on—was memorialized by Charles Moore, whose photograph later appeared in a two-page spread in *Life* magazine. Although it is an unposed picture, the sheriffs had spent their lives practicing for the shot.

Hendrickson's book tells the story of these lawmen, all staunch defenders of the law of segregation. Hendrickson also tells the stories of James Meredith and his family as well as the children of the seven sheriffs, through the eyes of the legacy that segregation has left them. Finally, Hendrickson looks at the next generation, the grandchildren, and explores whether the chains of that legacy have finally been broken. He explores the notion of a photograph as capturing a moment in time and then seeks to find out whether that moment is an accurate portrayal of what these men truly were—were they really cogs in a racist, almost lawless bigoted wheel that continued to turn, or were they more than that: leaders and instigators?

The book opens with the chilling story of the murder of Emmett Till in 1955, setting the stage for the reader to understand notions of race and justice in Mississippi during the civil rights era. Emmett Till, a fourteen-year-old African American from Chicago, had arrived in Mississippi three days earlier to visit family. After he allegedly propositioned a White woman, he was kidnapped, brutally murdered, and discarded in the Tallahatchie River. His murderers were prosecuted, but the jury acquitted the White men. Deputy John Ed Cothran, one of the seven sheriffs depicted in Moore's photograph (with his back to the camera), retrieved the body from the river. Hendrickson describes Cothran as a morally ambivalent man who lets others do his dirty work. On the surface, it looks like Cothran upholds the law, but he is an essential part of a political machine that sustains apartheid. This type of deception could prove fatal to a southern Black in the 1960s. At that time, Blacks needed to know whether they were dealing with a segregationist sheriff who opposed violence or a sheriff who was a "virulent racist who would deny blacks the most basic rights and indeed encourage threats to their lives and property" (46). The difference between the two types of sheriffs "could, for a black man, mean life or death" (46).

Hendrickson gives an example of Cothran's two-faced deceptions. Cothran proudly tells the story of how after he testified before the jury in Tallahatchie County (where Till was murdered), he was accosted by an irate man from Tallahatchie County who shouted: "You testified for the nigger-loving prosecution, Cothran. Didn't matter though, did it? Up here in this county we never convict a white man for killing a nigger. That's why Tallahatchie's number one" (112). Two months later, Leflore County (where Till was abducted) convened a grand jury that refused to indict the perpetrators for kidnapping. Cothran ran into the same man in the courtroom lobby and smugly retorted: "Guess we don't indict them down here, do we? Now you tell me who's number one? Leflore's number one" (113). The implication is soundly made: The law is an illusion; although the courts appear to control the legal process, the true power resides in the hands of the sheriffs and the jurors.

This theater of illusion recurs during the admission of James Meredith to Ole Miss. One of the fascinating stories Hendrickson re-creates is the negotiation between the Mississippi governor and the U.S. Attorney General. When Moore snapped his photograph on September 25, 1962, James Meredith was not yet on campus. On September 10, the U.S. Supreme Court had ordered Ole Miss to admit Meredith. Publicly, Gov. Ross Barnett adamantly refused; however, privately, he began negotiations with Attorney General Robert Kennedy (RFK). Around the same time as the photo was being shot, Barnett and Kennedy were negotiating the amount of firepower and force that would be displayed on campus:

RFK: I will send the marshals ... and they will come with Mr. Meredith and ... I will have the head marshal pull a gun and I will have the rest of them have their hands on their guns and their holsters.

Barnett: General, I was under the impression that they were all going to pull their guns. This could be embarrassing ... Isn't it possible to have them all pull their guns?

RFK: I hate to have them all draw their guns ... Isn't it sufficient if I have one man draw his gun and the others keep their hands on their holsters?

Barnett: They all must draw their guns (145–146).

By the end of the week, almost 31,000 federal troops had mobilized around the campus. Tensions were running high. Two people died, and more than 370 marshals, soldiers, and civilians were injured. As the Communist youth newspaper *Komsomolskya Pravda*, published in Moscow, described: "All of this is being done merely to prevent 29-year old James Meredith from becoming the first Negro student at the University of Mississippi, so as not to stain the purity of the educational establishments of the state." (148)

When Hendrickson researched the book, only two of the sheriffs were alive: Cothran and Ferrell. Hendrickson spent hundreds of hours meeting with them and their families. He tells of John Ed's grandson and namesake who works at Home Depot and gets along well with the Black employees—maybe even better than with the White employees. The grandson tells of his difficulties in overcoming prejudice:

> I catch myself at work all the time. I'll say to one of my Black workers at the Depot in my department, "Listen, there's a Black guy over there in the next aisle in a blue shirt. Go help him." And I catch myself—but it's always after the fact. I say to myself, "Now, why'd you have to bring color into it? Why didn't you just say, 'Go help that customer in the blue shirt?'" Probably ... five years ago, I'd have said, or wanted to say ... "Go over and help that nigger standing over there, nigger, hear?" ... And don't get me wrong ... [W]e have blacks in Mississippi, and we have some niggers in Mississippi, in the same way that we have white people, and we have white trash here. But I don't use the word nigger anymore. Or I try not to. (192–193)

Later, Cothran's son proudly reports his progress. He tells Hendrickson that he sent a supervisor over to the next aisle to help a customer. Cothran told the supervisor, "You'll recognize him. He's about my build and he's got a blue cap on." He brags to Hendrickson: "That's all I said. I didn't say the guy was black. Proud of myself " (204). Cothran's son demonstrates the difficulty of changing attitudes toward race.

Sons of Mississippi is excellent background reading on racial prejudice in the South and the forces of resistance against integration. The first two sections of the book, in which Hendrickson introduces the seven sheriffs and tells the tale of integration at Ole Miss, contain excellent material. The last section, in which the sins of the fathers are visited on the children, is too long and too far removed from the original story. The reader starts to feel sympathy for the children and grandchildren, who are being subjected to this intense scrutiny simply because they are related to sheriffs pictured in *Life* magazine. Perhaps most sympathetic is James Meredith's introverted son, Joe, who just wants to be left alone, having suffered as the son of a prominent but eccentric civil rights hero. Joe recently received his PhD in finance from Ole Miss but he wants to remain anonymous. Of his father he says: "So you think of my father forty years ago at this school. First day of class, every student in his class wants to leave the classroom. Every day you go into the cafeteria at lunch, and you hear the taunting ... What I mean is, sometimes I think I know what my father felt" (283). The reader is left wondering whether much has changed over the last forty years. In the words of T. S. Eliot: "We had the experience but missed the meaning" (296).

Warriors Don't Cry. Melba Pattillo Beals. New York: Washington Square Press, 1994. 312 pp. $22.00 (cloth), $14.00 (paper).

EDDIE L. SMITH
University of Missouri–Kansas City

"For some people, success is climbing the ladder. But for me, and my culture, success is not falling off the ladder." This statement was made by Victoria Smith (personal communication, June 2003), an African American mother of six. Her words point to one of the problems surrounding race in the United States.

Warriors Don't Cry, by Melba Pattillo Beals, is an autobiography from her diary about her personal experiences during the integration of Central High School in Little Rock, Arkansas, in 1957. She was one of the nine Black teenagers, who wanted an opportunity for a better education and who were at the center of the controversy to integrate Central High School. They were referred to as the *Little Rock Nine*. Pattillo Beals pulls readers into her home and her personal thoughts during the more than thirty-five years after her first year at Central. *Warriors Don't Cry* is written from her personal diary; notes from her mother, Dr. Lois Pattillo; and newspaper clippings the two saved over the years. Ms. Pattillo Beals started this book at eighteen years old, but didn't finish it because she "could not face the ghosts that its pages called up." Now she can tell her story without bitterness, but with humility and gratefulness. She acknowledges the White people in Little Rock who bravely dared to step out, speak up, and give their best. As an educator, I feel privileged that she decided to share this part of her life, a time that can only be retold by one of the nine African American teenagers.

The nine African American students were chosen on the basis of scholarship, personal conduct, and health. The Little Rock Nine had much in common. Their parents were strict, no-nonsense people, working hard to own their homes and to provide a safe, stable life for their families. They were teachers and preachers, and some had well-established positions in other professions.

Pattillo Beals began the book with an account of the thirty-year reunion of the nine Black alumni. Unlike thirty years earlier, when Gov. Faubus dispatched the Arkansas National Guard to prohibit their entry; then-governer Bill Clinton was there to extend a warm welcome and to celebrate their reunion and thirty years of race relations. I am reminded of a scene in the movie "Driving Miss Daisy" when Jessica Tandy, the elderly White lady, was being driven by Morgan Freeman, the old Black chauffeur. As he was driving her to a social gathering, she blurted out "Things sure have changed for you colored folks." As he got out to open the door for her, he murmured, "Things haven't changed that much."

Patillo Beals describes the pain of re-entering Central High School, even in the presence of her eight friends and the dignitaries who were praising them for their heroism. The Little Rock Nine traveled from around the world to attend this reunion. Pattillo Beals is a communications consultant in San Francisco and the author of several books on public relations and marketing. Gloria Ray Karlmark, a magazine publisher, is a citizen of the Netherlands. Minnijean Brown Trickey, a Canadian citizen, is a writer, has six children, and lives on a farm. Earnest Green lives in New York and is the vice president of Shearson. Thelma Mothershed Wair is a teacher in Illinois. Dr. Terence Roberts is a professor at the University of California, Los Angeles. Carlotta Walls LaNier is a real estate agent in Denver, Colorado. Jefferson Thomas is a Defense Department accountant from California. Elizabeth Eckford is a social worker and the only one remaining in Little Rock.

The physical and psychological punishment endured by these teenagers in evident by

> Pattillo Beals's current road to recovery. Schools are places where students need to experience success academically, physically, and psychologically. When schools focus on affirming the cultures that students bring to school, the policies can provide the support students need to further develop themselves culturally, thus making choices that will support their pursuits. (Moses, 2002). It is increasingly more important for scholars to take a critical look at these issues and examine the policies and practices in schools in hopes of answering the question of

schooling success for students of color (Dixson 2003). There needs to be an analysis of the color-blind ideology that promotes and perpetuates a power differential along color lines. Without this analysis we will not be able to recognize certain injustices when they are in front of us (DuBois 1996).

The values of Little Rock became an intricate part of the city's educational institutions. Their core beliefs promised equality of opportunity, freedom from government constraint, and a society based on love and justice. It delivered lynch mobs and cruel economic oppression to racial–ethnic groups of different color while protecting the privileges of its White citizens (Stornello 1998).

Pattillo Beals felt safe as long as she was in her brown world and people with brown skin tone were around her. The plan to integrate Central High School created tension in the sepia-toned community of Little Rock. She was willing to face mean men with guns and hanging ropes, and to give up fun times with her friends, to make things better for everybody, but her friends didn't see it that way. She describes how she often could detect fear in the eyes of her mother and other family members. People within their own community would make comments regarding why they were willing to anger the 'White folks.' They didn't see how endangering the lives and jobs of others had anything to do with freedom. They lived in constant fear and apprehension of not knowing what was expected of them. As Pattillo Beals describes it, the problem with colored folks stepping over the line was that the line was invisible, and where there were defined lines of expectations, there existed dual policies within certain social institutions. She was convinced through the encouragement from her mother that integration was the right thing for her.

The Pattillo family was bombarded with hate calls, and their home and personal property were attacked by mobs. Gangs of gun-toting renegades from other states reportedly came to Little Rock to join the fight against segregation. The local churches in the Black community tried to organized and arrange for protectors from the church to help. On one particular occasion, the would-be protector telephoned Pattillo Beals's mother, stating that he wasn't certain he wanted to be seen at their home at the cost of endangering his own family. Rather than criticize the man, she understood his position and fear. She also believed, as her grandmother had taught her, that the most important person on her side was her heavenly Father.

As a young girl, Pattillo Beals often asked the question "When will we get our chance to be in charge?" and her grandmother would reply "In God's time." Her friends and her faith are what brought them through abusive days at Central High School. The oppression against a group of people was such that they were taught that if God didn't intervene, there was no hope.

Pattillo Beals's grandmother would explain to her the importance of being a warrior: Warriors don't cry, and warriors don't quit. Pattillo Beals was a pioneer in the struggle for human rights and, while counting the cost, her grandmother realized the price would be greater if the fight didn't continue. One of Grandmother

Peyton's statements to Pattillo Beals was "If one of us does not step forward to claim our rights, we are doomed to an eternal wait in hope those who would usurp them will become benevolent." The Pattillo women didn't break down in the face of trouble; they acted with courage and dignity.

As the time grew closer for the new school year to begin, Gov. Faubus predicted that blood would run in the streets if Blacks forced integration in the peaceful capital city of Little Rock. And Little Rock was not peaceful on the first day of school. There were hecklers and huge mobs of people, hurling insults and inflicting fear in the hearts of the teenagers. Oftentimes, the teenagers found themselves alone, facing these huge crowds of people screaming at them like mad dogs. Pattillo Beals describes the hecklers as lynch mobs. Faubus dispatched two hundred seventy Arkansas National Guardsmen to prevent nine Black students from entering Central High School.

During the summer, Pattillo Beals and her family would frequently visit their family in Cincinnati, Ohio. Often she would find herself daydreaming about the idea that integrating Central High School would be the first step in making Little Rock just like Cincinnati. Whenever she visited Cincinnati, White people would speak to her, and she didn't see signs like "Colored only." The day before their first day of school at a news conference, Pattillo Beals describes what she felt was the first time in her young life when she felt equal to White people. She was willing to do whatever it took to keep that equal feeling at all times.

The Dimensions of Life

Warriors Don't Cry is not an indictment on Central High School, the school system, the community, or society at large. Pattillo Beals doesn't implicate anyone; she simply tells about her experience as a part of the history of integration in the United States. Students of color attend segregated schools at a higher rate in 1998 than they did in 1954 ("Revisiting *Brown*" 1996). Desegregation has become a social theoretical ideal rather than a common practice.

This book softened the soil of my heart and gave me a readiness to hear the truth as well as a readiness to speak the truth about the current state of race relations in U.S. society. There is so much in my world to lure me to lesser loyalties, so many voices clamoring for my attention. *Warriors Don't Cry* brought forth a fresh, warm reminder of who I am and what I need to be doing.

To see where we are going as an American society, we need to look at where we have been and clear the trash that we regret from the past. Together, we need to look ahead, prioritize, and examine the things that are really worth our time and attention. As a nation, we need to search within ourselves and address the issues we really believe, issues that have become our convictions as a society. Looking back over the last fifty years or so is not a pleasant view. The real tragedy comes when we have done, and continue to do nothing, about our mistakes. If we are going to clear away the trash of social injustice that has become a part of the regret of our past, we all are going to have to address the things that need our attention. It's a matter of social ownership.

We gravitate toward people who are most like ourselves. Our backgrounds and the depth of our experiences are the things that we will project (Duiguid 2003). This is exactly where our nation finds itself in this time of life.

References

Dixson, Adrienne. 2003. "When Race Matters: Examining Race-Conscious Education Policy and Practice." *Educational Researcher* 32:39–43.

Diuguid, Lewis. 2003, Nov. 19. Purpose of the Media. University of Missouri–Kansas City.

DuBois, W. E. B. 1996. "Concepts of Race." In *The Oxford W. E. B. DuBois Reader*, edited by E. Sundquist. New York: Oxford University Press.

Moses, Michelle. 2002. *Embracing Race: Why We Need Race-Conscious Education Policy.* New York: Teachers College Press.

Stornello, Joseph. 1998. *Social Hegemony and Educational Inequality: Problems of Ideology and Knowledge in Historical Texts.* New York: John D. Calandra Italian American Institute.

"Revisiting *Brown*." 1999, April 29. *Time*, 42–44.

Brown v. Board of Education: A Civil Rights Milestone and Its Troubled Legacy. James T. Patterson. New York: Oxford University Press, 2001. 270 pp. $27.50 (cloth), $16.95 (paper).

THOMAS V. O'BRIEN
Ohio State University at Mansfield

In May 1954, when the U.S. Supreme Court declared in *Brown v. Board of Education of Topeka, Kansas* that the separation of the races in schools was illegal, many observers remarked that the ruling would stand as one of the Court's most important decisions of the 20th century. Since then, there have been hundreds—if not thousands—of books, articles, dissertations, theses, and papers that have discussed the decision. Entire courses on *Brown* have found their way into the college curriculum in history, political science, and education departments. Amidst all this study and comment, however, there has been one book, Richard Kluger's (1975) *Simple Justice*, that has stood out as the best researched and most thorough treatment of the history of *Brown*. Now a recently published book by James T. Patterson, entitled *Brown v. Board of Education: A Civil Rights Milestone and Its Troubled Legacy,* completes the story. Patterson's book joins *Simple Justice* and brings the *Brown* story forward into the 21st century.

The history leading up to *Brown* was told compellingly by Richard Kluger. Kluger worked full time for seven years to research and write his book. Beginning the story in Clarendon County, South Carolina, where one of the five cases that eventually comprised the *Brown* case was filed, and circling his narrative to other litigation settings, Kluger convincingly (and with wit) fleshed out and humanized the individuals involved in the major court cases that surrounded *Brown*. No slouch for details, Kluger made full use of primary and secondary sources and interviews, introducing and developing scores of characters involving plaintiffs, attorneys, judges, witnesses, social scientists, teachers, and students, and in some instances even their relatives.[1]

Kluger's thesis was that, belatedly, the Supreme Court came to realize the obvious inequalities and discriminatory effects of the doctrine of "separate but equal" laid out in the infamous 1896 decision, *Plessy v. Ferguson* (1896). Kluger demonstrated that the court did not come to this conclusion easily or gracefully, or on its own, but rather arrived there through the commitment of plaintiffs and efforts of the legal arm of the National Association for the Advancement of Colored People (the Educational and Defense Fund, referred to as *The Fund*), which persevered in the nation's courtrooms between 1935 and 1954 and beyond. Writing in the mid-1970s and reflecting the state of liberal White thought on the integration issue, Kluger concluded that *Brown* represented "nothing short of a reconsecration of American ideals" and signaled that the United States stood for more than anti-Communism and the protection of property interests. The justices who ruled unanimously against racial segregation, he continued, acted as the conscience of the nation and thus "restored to the American people some measure of the humanity that had been drained away in their climb to worldwide white supremacy" (Kluger 1975, 710).

Today, though respectful of this decision, most scholars and students of American race relations are far more sober about *Brown*'s message and impact. What is also apparent to some of us is that Kluger and his treatment of *Brown* have become part of the story. Kluger was one of the many intellectuals who believed in the power of racial integration to remove educational and societal obstacles that had stood between equal opportunity and America's minority populations. Segregation was discrimination and thus was the true enemy of full-class citizenship for Blacks.

Some 25 years after the publication of *Simple Justice*, James Patterson has now published *Brown v. Board of Education: A Civil Rights Milestone and Its Troubled Legacy*. Patterson's book is the first in a series entitled *Pivotal Moments in American History*. Working off of Kluger's (1975) foundation, Patterson picks up the story and brings the *Brown* story forward into the new century. It is Patterson's subtitle that provides the clue as to how he will evaluate the ruling. *Brown* was at least two things: a civil rights milestone that was followed by unprecedented opportunity and progress for people of color. At the same time, it became a source of frustration for many activists and liberals, who, like Kluger in the early 1970s, hoped that the decision would spark full and unconditional equality for Blacks.

Patterson is a self-described "on the one hand, on the other" historian,[2] and he openly acknowledges his ambivalence in assessing *Brown*'s legacy.

Although these factors could have led to a wishy-washy story, in this case it does not. Patterson provides a seasoned and balanced account of *Brown* that does not replace Kluger's classic monograph but rather completes it in a way that Kluger could not. Indeed, Patterson hits his stride at the very moment that Kluger stumbled.[3] Putting to use much of the relevant secondary source literature and sprinkling in primary sources in chapters 1–5, he retraces Kluger's story into the mid-1950s. Here he tells the story with eloquence while taking to into account some of the nuanced scholarship that has been published since 1975. Patterson's real contribution, however, comes in the second half of the book. Here, focusing on the case law that followed in the wake of *Brown*, he explains stories behind key cases interpreting *Brown*: *Griffin v. County School Board of Prince Edward County*, *Green v. County School Board of New Kent County*, *Alexander v. Holmes County Board of Education*, *Swann v. Charlotte-Mecklenburg County Board of Education*, *Keyes v. Denver School District No. 1*, *Milliken v. Bradley*, and *San Antonio Independent School District v. Rodriguez*. In cogent narrative, Patterson tells the story of the rise and fall of the Fund's school integration litigation between the mid-1960s and mid-1970s. Like Kluger, he does this convincingly, fleshing out the actors and making the legalese accessible to nonlawyers. Unlike Kluger, he does this dispassionately and in much less space. He follows up on earlier actors, such as Thurgood Marshall (whom he feels became somewhat complacent on the Supreme Court; 151), Kenneth Clark, Robert Carter, Earl Warren, and Warren Burger, and introduces and develops new players such as Demetrio Rodriquez, William Rehnquist, and sociologist James Coleman.

He also addresses the relationship between desegregation and school achievement and evaluates Michael Klarman's (1994) "backlash thesis." With regard to race and achievement, Patterson advises America to create extensive early-intervention programs that focus on strengthening the cognition of very young children (217). Patterson's advice makes some sense from a psychological viewpoint and a White, middle-class perspective. Helping young children of color—especially young, poor children of color—develop more fully their cognitive brain power in Head Start-like programs would most likely translate into better developed cognitive pathways and higher standardized test scores. Readers of *Educational Studies* may find this discussion interesting but incomplete. Would early intervention lead to full equality? Or might the legacy of White supremacy defy this logic and find more subtle ways to prevail, as it has done time and time again? Might not these programs only replace desegregation as the new pana-cea? Is it reasonable social policy, from a Black perspective, to weaken the bond between the child and parent in order to attain higher test scores? Patterson's analysis avoids critical questions of this sort in large part because of his focus on studies that come from authors from the moderate and conservative points on the political spectrum. In reaching his conclusions Patterson relies on a handful of studies conducted by James Coleman, Patrick Moynihan, Patrick Mosteller, Gary Orfield, Diane Ravitch, Stephan and Abigail Thernstrom, and Christopher Jencks. This reliance is helpful in recounting a bit of the history through the 1980s. However, nearly all of these authors casually accept standardized tests as valid measures of student achievement. In contrast, many of today's educational researchers and scholars see the standardized test not only as a means of measur-ing achievement but also as a tool to sort students and limit educational and so-cial mobility. Undoubtedly, several other studies—including conceptual work by Oakes (1985), Kohn (1999, 2000), and others—should have been consulted to temper Patterson's analysis.

Patterson's discussion of the backlash thesis also left this reader unsatisfied. The backlash thesis begins with the observation that although *Brown* may have had great symbolic value, it brought about racial desegregation in very few public schools be-tween 1954 and 1964 because of substantial resistance by White southern politicians and educators. The thesis contends that rather than *Brown* itself serving as a catalyst for racial change, the fanatical political reaction to the decision in the Deep South, Virginia, Arkansas, and North Carolina drew the nation's attention to race, which in turn led to the demise of Jim Crow. The backlash thesis argues that the civil rights movement of the 1960s did not require *Brown*, but the highly public and at times vio-lent massive resistance movement did. It was not *Brown*, but violent resistance to *Brown*, that in the short term slowed down and then in the long term changed race re-lations. With acts of overt racism against nonviolent Black and several key White protesters in the spotlight thanks to television, concerned northerners grew sympa-thetic with the Black civil rights movement and pressured federal politicians to speak out and legislate against White violence and Black oppression (Klarman 1994, 81–118). Patterson reviews and challenges the backlash thesis and concludes that *Brown* did *not* set back the advance of more progressive southern race relations in the 1950s and that in the 1960s the backlash backfired as Blacks, even angrier than resis-tant Whites, took to the streets to protest (114). Although this is logical, Patterson turns to no additional evidence that would sharpen his story. Had he consulted addi-tional sources he would have found evidence that suggests that, in several hot spots, there was an early crystallization of White defiance to the idea of racial desegrega-tion several years before the decision (O'Brien 1999). Moreover, his focus on the backlash thesis leads Patterson to neglect relevant works, some of which suggest that historians have *underestimated* the immediate effects of *Brown* on American race relations (Franklin & Collier-Thomas 2000). In spite of these shortcomings, the book's foundation remains solid and Patterson's account stands out as the best sequel to Kluger's *Simple Justice*.

There is one more topic broached in Patterson's book that might be of interest to readers of *Educational Studies*: his take on pre-*Brown* southern schooling for Blacks. In fact, it is very possible that Patterson's discussion and position on segregated pre-*Brown* schooling in the south (and post-*Brown* segregated schooling in the South until the late 1960s) will raise eyebrows among African-American revisionist educational historians. He acknowledges Black solidarity as an unintended result of segregation (26) and references the work of Vanessa Siddle Walker (1996) and others who contend that good preintegration all-Black schools helped African-American children reach their highest potential (9). In the end, however, he sides with scholars such as David Cecelski (1994) and Robert Margo (1990) and asserts that readers should:

> Dismiss nostalgia and recall the handicaps of most black schools prior to *Brown*; crowded, often leaky, tarpapered buildings; awful facilities, poorly educated, badly paid teachers. Thousands of black children, like those in Summerton, South Carolina, had to walk miles to school. (186)

Finally, is there anything in Patterson's conclusion that helps us get beyond the integration versus separate-but-equal debate, the racial test gap dilemma, and the troubled, protracted legal battles that played out (and continue to play out) in the wake of *Brown*? Does his careful study go beyond explaining past? Does he offer us any course for the future? In a word, yes. Patterson sees the Black legal campaign for equal educational opportunity in particular and for equal protection under the law in general as a conspicuous national achievement in terms of the law. Still, he finds that *Brown* moved beyond a legal edict and became lasting, more deeply successful, only in those places where other political and social elements surfaced to bolster the *spirit* of the decision. The type of leadership emanating in local and state government and the community proved to be the key to how much of *Brown* would penetrate the social and psychic fabric of racist communities across America that had routinized their allegiance to White supremacy. Activists, students, school officials, mayors, councilors, legislators, the media, and others had to step up publicly and embrace the message of *Brown*, and the inappropriate reaction to it, in order for equal opportunity to be realized in day-to-day life. The law can set society in the right direction (or, for that matter in the wrong direction), but it is up to the rest of us—in whatever capacities we hold—to finish the work of fighting for and providing equal opportunity for all. Patterson's final call offers us the hope, sets forth the challenge, and outlines the blueprint for social change.

Notes

1. One reviewer, who was less than enthusiastic about this, lamented that Kluger used too much space attending to detail and elaborating on secondary characters (Conot 1976, 3).

2. Patterson made this remark during a panel discussion of his book at the History of Education Society Meeting in New Haven, CT, 18 October 2001.

3. One reviewer of *Simple Justice* wrote that in "an epilogue that mars the book, Kluger deals inadequately with the twenty years of late, and of racial turmoil and progress that have followed *Brown*" (Todd 1976, 110).

References

Brown v. Board of Education of Topeka, 347 U.S. 483 (1954).

Cecelski, David. 1994. *Along Freedom Road: North Carolina and the Fate of Black Schools in the South*. Chapel Hill: University of North Carolina Press.

Conot, Robert. 1976, January 18. "How Separate Became Equal." *New York Times Book Review*.

Franklin, V. P., and Bettye Collier-Thomas. 2000. *My Soul Is a Witness: A Chronology of the Civil Rights Era, 1954–1965*. New York: Henry Holt.

Klarman, Michael J. 1994. "How Brown Changed Race Relations: The Backlash Thesis," *Journal of American History* 81:81–118.

Kluger, Richard. 1975. *Simple Justice: The History of* Brown v. Board of Education *and Black America's Struggle for Equality*. New York: Knopf.

Kohn, Alfie. 1999. *The Schools Our Children Deserve: Moving Beyond Traditional Classrooms and "Tougher Standards"*. Boston: Houghton Mifflin.

Kohn, Alfie. 2000. *The Case Against Standardized Testing: Raising Scores and Ruining Schools*. Portsmouth, N.H.: Heinemann.

Margo, Robert. 1990. *Schooling and Race in the South, 1880–1950: An Economic History*. Chicago: University of Chicago Press.

Oakes, Jeannie. 1985. *Keeping Track: How Schools Structure Inequality*. New Haven, Conn.: Yale University Press.

O'Brien, Thomas V. 1999. *The Politics of Race and Schools: Public Education in Georgia, 1900–1961*. Lanham, Md.: Lexington Books.

Plessy v. Ferguson, 163 US 537 (1896).

Siddle Walker, Vanessa. 1996. *Their Highest Potential: An African American School Community in the Segregated South* Chapel Hill: University of North Carolina Press.

Todd, Richard. 1976, February. "Landmark." *Atlantic Monthly*, 237:109–110.

MEDIA REVIEW

The Road to *Brown*: The Untold Story of "The Man Who Killed Jim Crow." William Elwood, Producer. Mykola Kulish, Director. San Francisco: California Newsreel, 1989. 50 minutes, $199 (VHS only).

LYNN W. ZIMMERMAN
Purdue University–Calumet

Brown v. Board of Education of Topeka, Kansas, is the landmark Supreme Court decision that shaped the fight for equality and equity in all areas of life in the United States during the second half of the 20th century. The initial effect of the decision was to desegregate schools in an attempt to end racial discrimination in education. Its subsequent effects were to end racial segregation in transportation, housing, dining, employment, and all other aspects of American life. It was the legal backbone of the civil rights movement, which worked toward racial integration and ending racial discrimination. In addition to its impact on race relations in the United States, the *Brown* decision is the foundation upon which legislation for persons with disabilities and students with special needs have been based. The *Brown* decision is often viewed as a monolithic moment in time. However, the decision was the result of many years of build-up and hard work to create the social and legal climate that allowed for such a decision to be made.

"The Road to *Brown*" chronicles events leading up to the *Brown* decision in 1954. Framed by the life story of African American lawyer Charles Hamilton Houston, "The Road to *Brown*" examines the legal bases of racial segregation in the United States and the legal battles that were fought to end it. Houston is a little-remembered African American attorney who made overturning Jim Crow laws his life's work. This film highlights the pivotal role that African Americans played in bringing about legislation that ended legal segregation in the United States. African American authorities, such as the Hon. A. Leon Higginbotham, Jr.; Genna Rae McNeil, Houston's biographer; the Hon. Juanita Kidd Stout, Houston's former legal secretary; and Juanita Mitchell, former Youth Secretary of the National Association for the Advancement of Colored People (NAACP), lend their voices to giving Houston's work toward "killing" Jim Crow the credit it deserves.

Charles Hamilton Houston was born in 1895 in Washington, DC, of professional middle-class parents. His mother was a teacher, and his father was a lawyer. Thanks to his privileged background, Houston was able to attend a high school that prepared young African American men for college. He graduated summa cum laude from Amherst College in Massachusetts in 1915. Houston served as an officer in the American Expeditionary Force in World War I. His experiences in the segregated military during the war created a passion in Houston to fight injustices in a society that expected African American men to fight for a country that subjected them to racism, prejudice, and discrimination.

Houston graduated from Harvard Law School and worked to use the law to fight for true equality before the law for African Americans. He believed that one important issues was the underrepresentation of African Americans in the legal profession, resulting in a lack of adequate protection under the law for African Americans. In 1929, there were fewer than one hundred African American lawyers to represent nine million African American southerners. As dean of Howard University Law School, Houston addressed this shortage by improving the quality of education at Howard and by recruiting more African American law students. He also recruited young African American lawyers to work with him who had a zeal for social justice—young men such as Thurgood Marshall, Oliver Hill, and William Hasty.

Working as the special counsel for the NAACP, Houston decided that the battle for racial equality could best be fought in schools. He believed that a two-stage attack would be the most effective. The first stage would be to file precedent cases to make African American schools equal to White schools under the provisions of the "separate but equal" doctrine. Once this groundwork was laid, he then intended to attack segregation.

The doctrine of "separate but equal" has historical roots from the earliest days of America. Colonial laws and the U.S. Constitution defined slaves as property, not as people. In 1857, the *Dred Scott* decision declared that slaves were not citizens of any state, which upheld and reaffirmed the Constitution. This action set the stage for the Civil War. After the war ended in 1865, amendments were passed to the Constitution giving African American men citizenship rights equal to White men. The 13th Amendment abolished slavery, the 14th Amendment provided for equal protection under the law, and the 15th Amendment guaranteed the right to vote. However, in 1877, when federal troops pulled out of the South, southern states passed state laws that were designed to circumvent the all three amendments. The *Plessy v. Ferguson* case of 1896 challenged separate facilities for Blacks and Whites. Using the 14th Amendment as the basis, the Supreme Court ruling established the doctrine of "separate but equal." This ruling opened the door for the Jim Crow laws, which legally established separate public facilities for Blacks and Whites. These facilities were always separate but rarely equal. Twenty-one states passed laws that segregated everything from drinking fountains to schools. Houston, who is called "the man who killed Jim Crow," made it his life's work to destroy these laws. He believed that the administration of law and a legal campaign were the weapons to fight the lack of justice in the segregated United States.

To support his cause, Houston made a film in 1934 that documented the conditions of Black schools in the South. He used this information to substantiate the inequalities between Black and White school systems, showing that expenditures, facilities, and teacher salaries for Blacks were far behind those of White schools and White teachers. He also began to assemble court cases to establish precedents for the coming larger battle.

Finally, Houston was ready with his test case, *Murray v. Maryland*. Murray, a young Black man, had been denied admission to the University of Maryland Law School on the basis of race, even though this was the only law school in Maryland. The court ordered that he be admitted. Quickly following this victory, Houston presented a number of teacher salary cases, also in Maryland. African American teachers received increased salaries, and this decision prompted more cases in other southern states.

In the *Gaines v. Missouri* case, Gaines was denied admission to the only law school in Missouri. The court ruled that he could as easily attend schools in neighboring states that did admit Blacks. Houston appealed to the Supreme Court, which ruled that states could not provide equal education outside of their jurisdiction. Further cases reflected the changes that were beginning to take place. In *Sweat v. Painter*, the Supreme Court ruled that building a separate law school for a Black student was a violation of Sweat's 14th Amendment rights because a school is more than a building. The Supreme Court ruled in *McLaurin v. Oklahoma Regents* that students could not be segregated within the institution once admitted. McLaurin had been admitted to graduate school but was forced to sit in the hall while the White students sat in the classroom.

As the legal campaign gained momentum, Houston left the NAACP in 1940 so that he could devote all of his time to amass precedents in the areas of education, transportation, and labor. He sued to integrate the armed forces and defense industries after World War II. He also was active in protests and rallies around the country. Finally, the stress of his 16- to 18-hour days caught up with him, and he died at age 54 on April 22, 1950.

The fight Houston had begun did not end with his death. Houston's team, now led by Thurgood Marshall, chief counsel of the NAACP Legal Defense Fund, was ready to put forth the case that because separate could never be equal, segregation must be abolished. This case, first brought before the Supreme Court on December 9, 1952, was actually five separate cases that were presented under one heading, *Brown v. Board of Education of Topeka, Kansas*. Marshall's team faced arguments from John W. Davis, a formidable world-famous legalist. Marshall's argument was that separate schools marked Black children with a stamp of inferiority and that the subsequent suffering was opposed to the rights provided by the 14th Amendment.

Davis based all of his arguments on the *Plessy* case, believing that all precedents were on his side. On May 17, 1954, the Supreme Court handed down the unanimous decision that:

> to separate children solely because of their race generates a feeling of inferiority that may affect their hearts and minds in a way unlikely ever to be undone. In the field of education, separate but equal has no place. Separate educational facilities are inherently unequal.

The fight was not over once the *Brown* decision was reached. A number of states resisted integration, especially in the South, which also saw a resurgence of the Ku Klux Klan. However, the team of lawyers assembled by Houston continued the battle to end segregation, carrying it into other aspects of life and society, such as housing, restaurants, and public transportation, using *Brown* as their precedent. The civil rights movement grew out of these legal decisions and brought about other legal changes, including the Civil Rights Act of 1964 and the Voting Rights Act of 1965.

"The Road to *Brown*" is a powerful testament to a man and his work as well as an interesting and informative film about the fight for racial equality and equity in the United States. Narrated by Steven Anthony Jones, the film includes a wide variety of predominantly African American guests, including educators, lawyers, and civil rights activists, who give their perspectives on Houston and on the events leading up to the *Brown* decision.

Adding to the power and authenticity of the film are clips from Houston's 1934 film, other historical footage, and many still shots. Music is also effectively used to give support to the ideas and events in the film. "Strange Fruit," sung by Billie Holiday, is played as scenes of violence and lynching are shown, reinforcing the horror of these acts. Songs such as "No More Auction Block for Me, " "Freedom Land, " "No More Jim Crow, " "We Shall Overcome, " and "Oh Happy Day" remind viewers of the hope and joy with which these social and legal changes were awaited and greeted.

Civil rights laws can and have changed the quality of life in America and have changed the political balance of power in the United States. However, as Donald Watkins, an African American lawyer who is active in the Alabama state government, reminds viewers, the laws are meaningless unless they are supported and upheld. Although legal segregation has ended, de facto segregation—and, consequently, discrimination—still exists in many areas, and so there is still work to be done to provide equality for all Americans.

TIME EXPOSURE

Civil Rights March on Washington, August 28, 1963

Although the 1954 *Brown v. Board of Education of Topeka, Kansas,* decision(s) made racial equality the law of the land, its full implementation took several decades; some people argue that even today the process is far from complete. Inspired by demonstrations throughout the South earlier in the year, 250,000 people, mostly African Americans, descended on the National Mall in Washington, DC, on August 28, 1963, to demand equal rights for Blacks. The march is most remembered for two things: Roy Wilkins's announcement at the beginning of the assembly on the Mall that the previous day the great social activist W. E. B. DuBois had died in Ghana, and Martin Luther King's "I Have a Dream" speech—certainly the

The Civil Rights march on Washington, DC, August 28, 1963, showing a procession of African Americans carrying signs for equal rights, integrated schools, decent housing, and an end to bias. Photographer: Warren K. Lefler, 1963. Courtesy of the Library of Congress.

most important speech of the civil rights movement and a defining moment in American history.

Many different types of signs—both handmade and mass produced—were carried in the protest. Groups such as the United Auto Workers produced signs with slogans such as "UAW Says Jobs and Freedom for Every American," and a young Black woman carried a sign reading "Not 'Negroes' but AfroAmericans! We must Be Accorded Full Rights as Americans Not in the Future but Now." The photograph included above, taken by Warren K. Lefler, shows protestors with some of the mass-produced placards that were carried in the march, including ones that demanded "Equal Rights," "Integrated Schools," "Ending Bias," and "Decent Housing."

To explore earlier works in the Time Exposure Series visit the Time Exposure site:

Time Exposures: Visual Explorations in the History of American Education
http://www.education.miami.edu/ep/Time%Exposures/

EUGENE F. PROVENZO, JR.
University of Miami

BOOKS AVAILABLE LIST

BOOKS RECEIVED SPRING 2004

Brain, John F. *The Natural Bible for Modern and Future Man: The Ultimate Theology of the Still Evolving Mind.* Lanham, Md.: Rowman and Littlefield Publishing Group, 2004. 194 pp. $25.00 (paper).

Campbell, Jim, Leonidas Kyriakides, Daniel Muijs, and Wendy Robinson. *Assessing Teacher Effectiveness: Developing a Differentiated Model.* London: Routledge Falmer, 2004. 228 pp. $129.95 (cloth), $39.95 (paper).

Cohen, Sophia. *Teachers' Professional Development and the Elementary Mathematics Classroom: Bringing Understandings to Light* Mahwah, N.J.: Lawrence Erlbaum Asso - ciates, 2004. 190 pp. $49.95 (cloth), $19.95 (paper).

Conrad, Cecilia A., ed. *Building Skills for Black Workers: Preparing for the Future Labor Market.* Lanham, Md.: Rowman and Littlefield Publishing Group, 2004. 176 pp. $58.00 (cloth), $27.00 (paper).

Dembo, Myron H. *Motivation and Learning Strategies for College Success: A Self-Man- agement Approach* (2nd ed.). Mahwah, N.J.: Lawrence Erlbaum Associates, Inc., 2004. 304 pp. $55.01 (cloth), $34.50 (paper).

Gaztambide-Fernández, Rubén A. and James T. Sears, eds. *Curriculum Work as a Public Moral Enterprise.* Lanham, Md.: Rowman and Littlefield Publishing Group, 2004. 160 pp. $65.00 (cloth), $22.95 (paper).

Gonzales, Linda Dawson. *Sustaining Teacher Leadership: Beyond the Boundaries of an En- abling School Culture.* Lanham, Md.: Rowman and Littlefield Publishing Group, 2004. 164 pp. $29.00 (paper).

Hamilton, Andrea. *A Vision for Girls: Gender, Education, and the Bryn Mawr School.* Balti- more: John Hopkins University Press, 2004. 235 pp. $39.95 (cloth).

Hammack, Floyd M., ed. *The Comprehensive High School Today.* New York: Teachers Col- lege Press, 2004. 168 pp. $48.00 (cloth), $22.95 (paper).

Monteith, Moira, ed. *ICT For Curriculum Enhancement.* Bristol, UK: Intellect, 2004. 160 pp. $39.95 (paper).

Paley, Vivian Gussin. *A Child's Work: The Importance of Fantasy Play.* Chicago: University of Chicago Press, 2004. 111 pp. $19.00 (cloth).

Peters, Michael A., and Nicholas C. Burbules. *Poststructuralism and Educational Research.* Lanham, Md.: Rowman and Littlefield Publishing Group, 2004. 128 pp. $59.00 (cloth), $19.95 (paper).

Schweber, Símone A. *Making Sense of the Holocaust: Lessons From Classroom Practice.* New York: Teachers College Press, 2004. 185 pp. $44.00 (cloth), $19.95 (paper).

Sexton, Robert F. *Mobilizing Citizens for Better Schools.* New York: Teachers College Press, 2004. 144 pp. $44.00 (cloth), $18.95 (paper).

Sim, Stuart, ed. *The Routledge Companion to Postmodernism* (2nd ed.). London: Routledge Falmer, 2004. 401 pp. $104.95 (cloth), $22.95 (paper).

Sirotnik, Kenneth A., ed. *Holding Accountability Accountable: What Ought to Matter in Public Education.* New York: Teachers College Press, 2004. 216 pp. $44.00 (cloth), $19.95 (paper).

Wolf-Wendel, Lisa, Twombly, Susan B., and Suzanne Rice. *The Two-Body Problem: Dual-Career-Couple Hiring Practices in Higher Education.* Baltimore: John Hopkins University Press, 2003. 296 pp. $42.00 (cloth).

Wragg, E. C. *Education, Education, Education: The Best Bits of Ted Wragg.* London: Routledge Falmer, 2004. 172 pp. $96.95 (cloth), $22.95 (paper).

For a complete listing of Books Available for review, go to: http://www3.uakron.edu/aesa/publications/books.html

CALL FOR PAPERS

Special Issue: How Social Foundations of Education Matters to Teacher Education: A Policy Brief
Guest Editor: Dan W. Butin, *Gettysburg College*

In a teacher education climate of increased accountability to outcome-based professional standards, there is no single policy-focused articulation of why and how social foundations matters to teacher education. This special edition of Educational Studies hopes to fill this gap. The goal is that this volume will serve as a stand-alone brief for the role and value of social foundations of education within teacher education. The social foundations field must of course be cognizant of the larger ongoing discussions concerning the viability of teacher education in the preparation of future teachers; nevertheless, it is vital that the field be able to articulate—to colleagues, department chairs, college deans, policymakers, external reviewers and examiners, and the public at large—a response to the question of "how (and why) does social foundations matter for teacher education?"

As such, this call for papers is for very specific and focused submissions. The topics are outlined below. Submissions may engage an entire topic (including sub-topics) or focus on one or more of the sub-topics only. Given the editor's desire to cover all of the topics, it is expected that submissions be no more than approximately 10 manuscript pages (longer submissions engaging an entire topic will be accepted). The editor is looking for theoretical perspectives, research (either new or reworked) and literature reviews of existing scholarship. Please contact Dan Butin for additional information, to discuss the stated topics, or to suggest additional topics for this special issue.

Manuscripts should be double spaced, using the *Chicago Manual of Style* documentation (see Contributor Information in this journal).

The submission deadline is *March 1, 2005*. Final decisions will be made by April 1, 2005. The journal is expected to be published by December, 2005.

Suggested Topics

1. What is social foundations of education?
2. How (and/or why) does social foundations matter for teacher education?
   a. Theoretical articulations

    b. What evidence do we have, other than theoretical, about how (and/or why) social foundations matters?

    c. What would count as evidence that social foundations matters to the preparation and practice of teachers, and what models of inquiry would generate evidence that would be compelling?

3. What are the "best practices" and/or exemplary models of social foundations within teacher education?

    a. Theoretical articulations

    b. Single-case studies

    c. Literature review

4. How does social foundations support and enhance teacher education programs?

    a. vis à vis NCATE?

    b. vis à vis INTASC?

    c. vis à vis NBPTS?

5. Research of the impact of social foundations on prospective teachers: outcome measures may include affective or cognitive changes, performance on newly mandated professional assessments of teacher knowledge and practice (e.g. PRAXIS), etc.

    a. Single-case studies

    b. Literature review

6. The historical role and context of social foundations within teacher education

Correspondence for this special issue should be addressed to Dan W. Butin, Assistant Professor of Education, Gettysburg College, P.O. Box 396, Gettysburg, PA 17325. Telephone: 1-717-337-6553; FAX: 1-717-337-6777. E-mail: www.gettysburg.edu/~dbutin or dbutin@gettysburg.edu

For Product Safety Concerns and Information please contact our EU
representative GPSR@taylorandfrancis.com
Taylor & Francis Verlag GmbH, Kaufingerstraße 24, 80331 München, Germany

www.ingramcontent.com/pod-product-compliance
Lightning Source LLC
Chambersburg PA
CBHW062043270326
41929CB00014B/2519